BAR CEL ONA

Travel with Marco Polo Insider Tips

INSIDER TIP
Your shortcut to a great experience

MARCO POLO TOP HIGHLIGHTS

BARRI GÒTIC ⭐
The winding streets of the Old Town take visitors back to the Middle Ages.
📷 *Tip: The alleys look particularly beautiful in the late afternoon light.*

➤ p. 30

PALAU DE LA MÚSICA CATALANA ⭐
Modernist architect Lluís Domènech i Montaner pulled out all the stops (photo).
📷 *Tip: The ceramic flowers that detail the columns and balustrades look great against a blurred background.*

➤ p.35 and p.107

LA RAMBLA ⭐
An open-air stage for tourists, flaneurs … and pickpockets – the unique charm of Barcelona's best-known promenade.

➤ p. 46

MUSEU PICASSO ⭐
An impressive collection housed within medieval walls pays homage to the genius painter – with first-rate special exhibitions.

➤ p. 37

MERCAT DE SANT JOSEP ⭐
It's for good reason that the "belly of Barcelona" is considered the city's most beautiful indoor market.
📷 *Tip: Food photographers should come first thing in the morning and ask for permission – before the tour groups descend.*

➤ p. 77 and p. 90

CASA MILÀ ☆

The city's wildest apartment block sets new standards for housing. You won't get closer than this to the genius that was Gaudí.

➤ p. 42

SAGRADA FAMÍLIA ☆

Gaudí's unfinished masterpiece is Barcelona's most famous building site.

📷 *Tip: The best way to capture the sheer scale is to use a wide-angle lens from the middle strip of Avinguda Gaudí.*

➤ p. 43

MUSEU NACIONAL D'ART DE CATALUNYA ⑨

From frescoes to photography: this collection is one of a kind.

📷 *Tip: Linger until evening when the staircase puts the magical lights of the Font Màgica into perspective.*

➤ p. 54

PARK GÜELL ⑧

As well as the dragons, butterflies, snakes and magical grottos, Gaudí's fairy-tale garden offers a fantastic view out over the city.

➤ p. 58

CAMP NOU ⑩

Impressive stadium home to the club that means so much more to the city than just football.

➤ p. 111

CONTENTS

Symbol	Description	Symbol	Description
⏱	Plan your visit	☂	Rainy day activities
€–€€€	Price categories	🐷	Budget activities
(*)	Premium-rate phone number	👥	Family activities
		⚑	Classic experiences

(📖 A2) Refers to the removable pull-out map
(📖 a2) Refers to the inset street map on the pull-out map
(0) Located off the map

CONTENTS

BEST OF
BARCELONA

The towers of the Sagrada Família offer incredible views

BEST ☂
WHEN IT RAINS

ACTIVITIES TO BRIGHTEN YOUR DAY

MEDITATIVE ATMOSPHERE

Santa Maria del Mar is the favourite church of the Barcelonians – and for good reason. You can either sit in the simple church and enjoy the peace, or listen to a concert with excellent acoustics.

➤ p. 38, Sightseeing

CATALAN CULTURE

A rainy day allows you plenty of time to admire the world-famous collection of Romanesque frescoes alongside exhibitions on Renaissance, Baroque and contemporary painting and photography at the *Museu Nacional d'Art de Catalunya*.

➤ p. 54, Sightseeing

GAUDÍ FOR CONNOISSEURS

Who has time for the beach when you're in a city this rich in Modernist treasures? You may as well make the most of it and visit one of the lesser-known Modernist jewels such as *Casa Vicens*, Gaudí's first major commission, complete with impressive murals.

➤ p. 58, Sightseeing

INDULGE YOUR SWEET TOOTH

Caught in a shower in the Old Town? Take refuge in one of the many pretty cafés, such as *Caelum* (photo) in a corner house near Santa Maria del Pi. This lovingly designed eatery dishes up delicacies from Spain's monasteries. Enjoy coffee and cake in the warmth and watch the rain patter against the windows.

➤ p. 86, Shopping

RELAX IN THE ROMAN BATHS

If you're going to get wet, you may as well do it properly! The Arab baths at *Aire de Barcelona* give you a chance to relax under the stylishly renovated vaults. And sweet tea and a massage will surely dispel any lingering annoyance at the disappointing weather.

➤ p. 112, Active & relaxed

BEST ON A BUDGET

FOR SMALLER WALLETS

AN EVENING OF PICASSO

Picasso's works fetch eye-watering prices, but you can enjoy his art for free at the *Museu Picasso* (photo) if you book a ticket online for Thursday evening or the first Sunday of the month. Admission for the *Museu Nacional d'Art de Catalunya* is also free on the first Sunday of each month.
➤ p. 37 and p. 54, Sightseeing

MODERNISM IN THE TEMPLE OF FASHION

If you visit every Modernist building in Barcelona, you'll soon rack up a pretty hefty bill. Instead, why not take a look at the *Massimo Dutti flagship store* at 69 Passeig de Gràcia. The 1902 *piano nobile* has been lavishly restored – the ornate filigree fireplace is absolutely stunning.
➤ p. 40, Sightseeing

A PORTION OF GOURMET

If tapas are your thing, you can visit the creators of the world's fifth best restaurant without bankrupting yourself. At *Compartir*, the famous trio Oriol Castro, Eduard Xatruch and Mateu Casañas dish up Mediterranean delicacies.
➤ p. 72, Eating & drinking

JAMMING WITH THE STARS OF TOMORROW

Whether you're into flamenco, jazz or pop, you'll enjoy the show at the *JazzSí Club,* where students of the Taller de Músics demonstrate their skills every evening. Tickets cost between eight and ten euros, which is more than fair, especially as it includes your first drink.
➤ p. 103, Nightlife

SPONTANEOUS SAVINGS

Concert, theatre and opera tickets are all half price three hours before the curtain goes up at the *Tiquet Rambles* in the Palau de la Virreina.
➤ p. 140, Good to know

BEST WITH CHILDREN

FUN FOR YOUNG & OLD

AMONG SHARKS

Test your courage at the *Aquàrium*: can you look a shark in the eye without batting an eyelid in the 80m-long underwater tunnel? Marvel at 450 different animal species across 35 tanks – there's so much to discover as the aquarium is structured to reflect the world's seven seas.
➤ p. 51

FOR SWIMMERS & SUN WORSHIPPERS

Dig in the sand, enjoy the waves and captain your own pirate ship on the climbing frames – kids are always happy with an afternoon at the *beach*. Catering is also a breeze thanks to a range of nearby restaurants, ice cream parlours and mini supermarkets. Oh, and pack a volleyball – the city puts up nets in the summer.
➤ p. 51

PLAY THE EXPLORER

In *CosmoCaixa*, Barcelona's science museum, you can walk through a tropical rainforest, look at the stars or create a sandstorm. Hands-on areas and the planetarium are great fun.
➤ p. 61

FEAST LIKE HARRY POTTER

It must be magic! Even the fussiest of eaters will be converted by *Harry Potter*-themed café *Pudding*. The walls are hung with the house coats of arms the pillars have been transformed into tree trunks from the Forbidden Forest and kids will be happy to munch on cheesecake and bagels.
➤ p.69

WAY UP HIGH

A trip in the *Teleféric* isn't for the faint-hearted! The cable car up Montjuïc might give you butterflies but the panoramic views make it all worthwhile.
➤ p. 138

BEST

CLASSIC EXPERIENCES

ONLY IN BARCELONA

STONE REPTILE

Bones, masks and elephant feet: for his bizarre Art Nouveau *Casa Batlló*, on the chic Passeig de Gràcia, Catalan's most famous architect Antoni Gaudí turned to nature for inspiration. Once inside, no two rooms are the same.
➤ p. 41

GAUDÍ'S DIVINE TEMPLE

The *Sagrada Família* is Barcelona's world-famous landmark. Let the gigantic columns and spectacular interior of the huge nave work their magic on you – you haven't seen Barcelona if you haven't been here!
➤ p. 43

POPULAR PANOPTICON

Dive into the crowds of *La Rambla* and join tourists and theatregoers, culture seekers and kitsch vendors, stylish opera guests and dexterous waiters. Further down the Rambla, the living statues in their imaginative costumes are sure to catch your eye.
➤ p. 46

MEDITERRANEAN SPIRIT

Enjoy this Mediterranean metropolis while sipping a coffee or a cool beer on one of its many secluded squares. *Plaça de la Vila* and *Plaça de la Virreina* in Gràcia are particularly atmospheric.
➤ p. 58

BARCELONA IN APPETISING TITBITS

Follow the locals' tapas trail! Try the fish and seafood in the rustic *Bar Leo*, the rich choices of market-fresh tapas in *Cervecería Catalana* or the home-made tapas in *El Xampanyet*.
➤ p. 68 and p. 69

GET TO KNOW BARCELONA

Castellers build their human towers – much to the awe of those watching on

DISCOVER BARCELONA

Rippling like the Mediterranean: the wooden Rambla del Mar footbridge in the old harbour

Whether you're enjoying a hilltop picnic or a cocktail on the beach, visiting cultural venues or cool bars, sightseeing or shopping, you are guaranteed not to get bored in Barcelona. And don't forget the ever-present Mediterranean lifestyle – whatever the time of day and no matter how busy the people are, there is always time for an espresso or a drink. It's no wonder that there are cafés and bars on every corner, to accompany the countless exciting museums and quirky venues that are sometimes hidden behind metre-thick medieval ramparts.

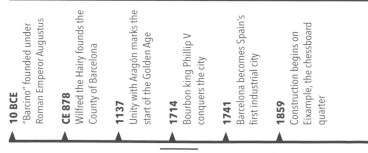

10 BCE
"Barcino" founded under Roman Emperor Augustus

CE 878
Wilfred the Hairy founds the County of Barcelona

1137
Unity with Aragón marks the start of the Golden Age

1714
Bourbon king Phillip V conquers the city

1741
Barcelona becomes Spain's first industrial city

1859
Construction begins on Eixample, the chessboard quarter

MEDIEVAL MEETS HYPERMODERN

You can gain a good overview of the fashionable metropolis from your plane as you approach the airport. The bit that looks from above like a huge, dark, unravelling ball of wool is the Barri Gòtic (Gothic quarter) with its winding alleyways. The streets here are so narrow that some don't see any sunlight at all, while others are illuminated by no more than a narrow strip. Away from the crowds of tourists you may still be able to discover a few secret nooks and crannies that feel as if they've come straight out of the Middle Ages. The only city with a larger old town is Naples. Alongside the Gothic quarter you can also see the razor-sharp grid plan of the Art Nouveau quarter Eixample, which looks like a chessboard dotted with hypermodern skyscrapers reaching towards the sky.

THE BEAUTY OF CHAOS

Amid the hustle and bustle of the Old Town, it's possible that you may suddenly pick up the sounds of a classical guitar or some smooth jazz. Particularly in the area around the cathedral you can find some genuinely talented buskers who play everything from classical to pop. A similarly harmonious blend of the historic and the modern can be found elsewhere in the Barri Gòtic too: Roman ruins rub shoulders with trendy concept stores; tiny bric-à-brac shops stand next to

INSIDER TIP
The soundtrack to the city

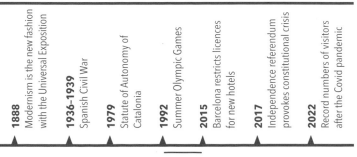

1888
Modernism is the new fashion with the Universal Exposition

1936–1939
Spanish Civil War

1979
Statute of Autonomy of Catalonia

1992
Summer Olympic Games

2015
Barcelona restricts licences for new hotels

2017
Independence referendum provokes constitutional crisis

2022
Record numbers of visitors after the Covid pandemic

fashionable boutiques. In other words, the people of Barcelona are familiar with contradictions. That was already the case when the city's rich residents erected one of the most magnificent Art Nouveau quarters in the world. Barcelona's high society wanted to show off their wealth, so the buildings had to be as ornate as possible – yet behind their splendid façades the occupants led relatively frugal lifestyles, with some malicious gossips accusing them of meanness. Even today, people in the rest of Spain make fun of Catalonians being penny-pinchers. Whether or not this cliché of the stingy Catalonian has any truth to it, money is clearly no object when it comes to the image of the region's biggest city. From architecture, design and fashion to art and culture, the people of Barcelona are happy to splash their cash and unwilling to do anything by half measures.

BARCELONA REINVENTS ITSELF TIME & AGAIN
This Mediterranean city has never been short of innovative energy. It is constantly on the move and reinventing itself. All it takes is some great event to prompt a pioneering enterprise that was waiting in the wings. It was like that for the World Exhibition of 1888, which awakened the city from its Sleeping Beauty slumber and heralded a new departure into an age of blossoming Art Nouveau. The grounds around the Ciutadella Park were created for this show. In 1929, parts of the city were again completely turned inside out to get ready for the second World Exhibition – this time it was the turn of Montjuïc.

The Olympic Games of 1992 then bequeathed to Barcelona a completely new city: the depressing heritage of 40 years of dictatorship was swept aside, and the revamped metropolis began its ascent to become a mecca for architects, urban planners and tourists. One of the most popular achievements was the miles-long sandy bathing beach. At the weekend in particular, Barcelonians stroll, jog, bike or skate along the palm-fringed promenade and treat themselves to a paella with sea view.

A HI-TECH QUARTER MAKES A NAME FOR ITSELF
North of the Olympic village, the Poblenou quarter is becoming a favourite spot among trendy city dwellers and young families thanks to its small-town charm. Imposing skyscrapers and chic headquarters belonging to media companies are springing up around Plaça Glòries, while the city's former traffic junction has been transformed into a spacious green park. The eye-catcher of this brave new architectural world is the huge phallic skyscraper of Torre Glòries – shimmering in red and blue, it was designed by Jean Nouvel. The top floor promises a breath-taking view of the city's new skyline.

A LONG HISTORY OF NATIONAL PRIDE
The Catalan propensity to grand gestures has its roots in history. In the 19th century, nothing was too ostentatious for the bourgeoisie, whether materially or

Carrer del Bisbe is at the heart of the Gothic quarter

intellectually, especially if it rivalled the unloved central power in Madrid. Even at that time, the economic powerhouse of Catalonia wanted to overtake politically dominant Castile – at least in art and architecture. Everything was supposed to be even bigger, more splendid and more beautiful than in the Spanish capital. Not much has changed since then; the thorn of history is still deeply embedded in the skin of Catalonia: once a medieval global power and prestigious trading centre, Catalonia has time and again had to accept central Spanish supremacy over the centuries. The architectural grandeur of the Gothic quarter, represented by masterpieces such as the cathedral or the Drassanes shipyard, attests to the glory days of Catalonia, which are still looked upon proudly today.

The foundation of the Catalan nation was laid in CE 878 by Count Wilfred the Hairy (Guifré el Pilós) who united several counties under one dynasty that reigned from the palace on Plaça del Rei. The principality's decline began at the end of the 15th century, when the crowns of Aragon and Castile were united through the marriage of the "Catholic kings" Ferdinand and Isabella. Catalonia's sun had set.

The Catalans made the "wrong" choice when they sided with the Habsburgs in the War of the Spanish Succession (1701–14), because when the Habsburgs eventually lost the war, Catalonia also lost most of its rights to self-governance. Bourbon troops laid siege to Barcelona for a year, until the city finally capitulated on 11 September 1714 and the vengeful victor, Phillip V, had part of Barcelona's Old Town razed to the ground. For Catalans, this date marks a day of national humiliation, and it is still a national day of remembrance.

More recently, Spain's dictator General Franco wanted to tidy up the rebellious bastion in the north and annihilate any sign of its identity, starting with the Catalan language, which was banned publicly. The Franco dictatorship may have ended in 1975, but its consequences still affect the Catalans. Although some 75 per cent of the population can now speak Catalan, a good half of the locals prefer Spanish in day-to-day life.

IN PERMANENT OPPOSITION TO MADRID

Distrust and prejudices of the Catalans towards the central government in Madrid – and vice versa, of course – can only be overcome gradually. There have been repeated upheavals, most recently in the autumn of 2017, when Spain slid into a major constitutional crisis following the unauthorised Catalan independence referendum. Anyone who has witnessed the impromptu mass gatherings and frenetic celebrations on the Rambla after a victory of F.C. Barcelona over arch-rival Real Madrid knows that this is about more than just football. Add to this the Catalan tendency to look towards Europe. The Catalans have always felt closer to their northern neighbours than to the Iberian Peninsula. Barcelona is often called the north's southernmost city or the northernmost metropolis of the south – and both are true.

It is a city of contrasts and sometimes these clash quite dramatically: in the lower part of the Old Town quarter of Raval, traces of the demi-monde of prostitutes, fraudsters and gangsters that inspired the French writer Jean Genet to write *The Thief's Journal* are still visible in the legendary Barri Xino, the port and red-light district of Barcelona; a few paces away, the hip cultural and bar scene around the Museum of Contemporary Art and the fancy new boulevard of Rambla del Raval transform the picture entirely.

COMPLAINTS ABOUT MASS TOURISM

Since the arrival of mass tourism, thousands of flats are being let to tourists via internet platforms such as Airbnb, and rents are skyrocketing. The city has tried to counteract this trend with restrictive licensing and hefty fines, but so far their attempts have failed. The fact that bustling Barcelona has become one of the world's most popular tourist hotspots has had a big impact on prices. But while Barcelona might cherish its stylish image, it is not a uniformly glossy modern metropolis. Many corners of the city still have shops and bars that have survived the design fever. And there are still enough young creatives living here with plenty of subversive imagination to challenge the emblematic *disseny barceloní*.

So, you will experience a city of exciting contrasts, always on the move – and always with a surprise up its sleeve. Don't be sad if you don't manage to take it all in. Just tell yourself: "next time!" Because when people leave Barcelona they are usually pretty sure that they'll be back.

AT A GLANCE

1,640,000
inhabitants

Most popular area to live is Eixample

9
UNESCO
WORLD HERITAGE
SITES

2,700
hours of sunshine per year

1,300 more than the UK average

4,780m
sandy beaches

The longest beach is Platja San Sebastià at 1.1km

8,000
wild parakeets live in Barcelona – more than any other Spanish city

1,300
IT start-ups

Ranked fifth in Europe

7
restaurant visits

per resident per month

ROME FROM ROME!

Barcelona has more motorbikes than any other European city – every third vehicle in fact.

FC BARCELONA
owned by 143,086 of its fans

Rival Real Madrid is owned by just 92,000

MOST POPULAR FIRST NAMES
Maria
Antonio

MOST EXPENSIVE AREA
SARRIÀ

UNDERSTAND BARCELONA

C-EXIT

The yellow ribbons fluttering from many a Barcelona balcony aren't just colourful street decorations. Instead, they're a sign of solidarity with all those who've had trouble with the judiciary because of Catalonia's struggles for independence. In fact, the desire for a separate state is nothing new in Catalonia. More than being an economic issue, most people in favour of independence, known as the *Independentistes*, are concerned with what they believe is a lack of respect. In their eyes, they are being bullied by the central government.

In 2010, a planned reform granting more political and financial independence to the region was nipped in the bud by the Spanish Constitutional Court. Tensions reached an all-time high in the autumn of 2017, when former President of Catalonia Carles Puigdemont held a vote on independence despite the ban from Madrid. Madrid sent in the police, and when the Catalan parliament proclaimed the "Free Republic of Catalonia" three weeks later, they accused the entire regional government of rebellion. This still rankles with many today.

CASTELLS

The traditional Catalan human "castles" often take the breath away of the uninitiated. The *castellers* construct their daring towers up to ten levels high (nearly 15m). Depending on the type of construction, the people stand in groups of four, three, two or alone on the shoulders of those below, and at the end a child climbs the "summit" and briefly raises their hand as a sign of victory. A popular sport and expression of Catalan national pride, these *castells* are a traditional part of any celebration. A perfect pyramid finishes with a seamless descent. This is how the *castells* are judged when the associations, *colles de castellers*, try to trump each other at competitions, to the sound of drum rolls and traditional Catalan music.

In Barcelona, *castellers* usually perform on the *Plaça de Sant Jaume* (see p. 33). The first towers were recorded in the late 17th century, when people climbed on each others' shoulders at the end of popular dances. From the 18th century, the dancers tried to surpass each other through ever more daring formations, and the dance element soon fell by the wayside.

The *castellers* experienced their heyday in the 19th century. As a symbol of Catalan national culture, they were banned during the military dictatorship under General Franco. Today the custom is again a staple of popular fairs and celebrations – and was even placed under UNESCO World Heritage protection in 2011.

⚑ At the *Castellers de Barcelona* association *(castellersdebarcelona.cat)* you can watch the training and, if you dare, you can even take part in building a pyramid – for free.

Toothless monster: the dragon in Park Güell definitely doesn't bite

MADMAN OR GENIUS?

A genius or a madman, that was one teacher's assessment of Antoni Gaudí as a young student of architecture. Visitors to buildings by this master architect and craftsman might come to the conclusion that both are true. Born the son of a coppersmith in 1852 in Reus near Tarragona, Gaudí moved away rapidly from the path of the architecture of his time as it was taught at university. The organic forms of his buildings, their fantastic colours and the exuberant imagination of his utopian designs upset many of his contemporaries. It's hardly surprising that all his life he was short of official commissions and awards. Instead, it was private patrons of the arts such as Eusebi Güell who recognised Gaudí's genius and supported his work – today, Park Güell, Palau Güell and Casa Milà

form part of the UNESCO World Heritage list.

Gaudí's life was full of contradictions. As a young man, he had a reputation for being a dandy who enjoyed life to the full, was enthusiastic about revolutionary ideas and moved in atheist circles. Despite this, at the age of 31 he started building the Sagrada Família church, which is still unfinished today. In his latter years he dedicated all his creative energy to the church and lived an increasingly ascetic life. In 1926, the "Dante of architecture" was killed by a tram.

SHARING IS CARING

"I'll repair your toilet flush in return for an hour of English tuition." Offers of this kind are not unusual in Barcelona, as the international trend towards the

APERITIUS

SARDINETES EN OLI		4,50
ESCOPINYES		7,75
SEITONS	2,25	3,75
MUSCLOS		3,95
XIPIRONS		5,25
NAVALLES		6,55
LANGOSTILLOS		3,60
CLOÏSSES		6,50
ANXOVES	3,00	5,00
OLIVES		1,00
PATATES		1,00

TENS FRED?
MINIFONDUES

PROPOSTES DEL DIA
CUIXETA DE GUATLLA
+ COPA DE VI NEGRE 3,65

Do you understand Catalan? Knowing the basics will help you decode menus

sharing economy has long been familiar to its inhabitants. During the 1970s, neighbourhood associations began to organise *bancos del tiempo* – "time banks" – where neighbours could exchange repair work for tuition, or babysitting for a cooked meal. Who needs money when you have time and talent? This *modus operandi* has since been picked up by the city administration which, under the aegis of left-wing mayor Ada Colau, promoted time banks as a sustainable economic concept.

CATASPANISH

Officially, Catalonia is bilingual: all notices, forms, signposts, etc. are supposed to be written both in Spanish and in Catalan. In practice, the Catalans prefer their own language to Spanish, which can sometimes cause confusion. But if you react to a question or a greeting in Spanish, Catalan-speakers will usually automatically switch to Spanish. Catalan (in varying dialects) is spoken by around six million people all along the Mediterranean coast between Perpignan and Alicante, in the Balearics, in Andorra – and in the Sardinian town of Alghero.

UNDERGROUND

If you suddenly find yourself looking at a row of well-maintained gravestones while shopping in the Gothic quarter, don't worry, you haven't taken a wrong turn – you've just come across the excavations on the Plaça de la Vila de Madrid. Located just a short stroll away from La Rambla, with its streetwear and lingerie shops, this is where the Romans buried their dead. There were once 70 graves buried in this necropolis, and when Roman Emperor Augustus founded the colony of *Barcino* over 2,000 years ago this settlement of up to 1,000 people also included a temple, a forum, a bathhouse and workshops. If you want to see what it once looked like, head down to explore the subterranean Roman ruins at the *Museum of City History (see p. 30)*.

AGAINST THE GRAIN

Modernisme, the Catalan variant of Art Nouveau, which entered the scene in the late 19th century, was not only the expression of rebellion against the geometry and straight lines of an industrial society. Most of all, it offered a suitable aesthetic framework for the spirit of the upwardly mobile bourgeoisie. In decoratively exuberant designs, the Catalan bourgeoisie – wealthy but politically dominated by Madrid – found an effective means of occupying the public stage and promoted their own national style to mirror Catalans' reawakening confidence.

The movement was not restricted to architecture, but encompassed all areas of design, whether furniture, ceramics, jewellery or cast-iron. Its main protagonists were Josep Puig i Cadafalch, Lluís Domènech i Montaner and Antoni Gaudí.

TRUE OR FALSE?

NORTHERN EUROPEANS OF THE SOUTH

If you're looking for a sure-fire way to insult a Barcelonian, tell them how great you find it here in Spain, then blast out Manolo Escobar's 1970s hit "Que viva España". Barcelona hates being lumped in with the rest of Spain, and the Catalans have always felt more at home with northern Europe than the south. Culturally, they value reliability and entrepreneurial thinking and are quite happy to be stereotyped as serious and reserved. That said, over-punctuality doesn't go down well either. The Catalans and Barcelonians are not just the northern Europeans of the south, but somehow also the southern Europeans of the north …

GAME OF EXTREMES

Sensible or off their rocker? Actually, the city's inhabitants are often both at once. This symptomatic mix is known as *seny i rauxa*, an odd mix of a good dash of common sense on the one hand and a frenetic tendency to let everything get rather out of hand on the other. For Barcelona, this has often been a blessing in disguise and an interplay that has achieved economic prosperity while paving the way for artistic geniuses like Antoni Gaudí and Salvador Dalí.

To gain an overview of the movement, why not follow the *Ruta del Modernisme (www.rutadel modernisme.com)* put together by the tourist board. It will take you not only to the main sites, but also to hidden Modernist gems such as pharmacies, libraries or general stores.

RED-LIGHT RESEARCH

Although Pablo Picasso was born in 1881 in Málaga in southern Spain, he is also considered a son of the city of Barcelona, having lived and worked here for nine years. In fact, perhaps the most famous artistic genius of the 20th century is said to have declared that it was in Barcelona where he discovered what he was capable of. The boy moved to the city in 1895, when his father got a job as teacher at La Llotja art academy. Even then, the artistic talents of the young Picasso were so obvious that he was accepted at the academy aged only 13. When he was 14, young Pablo got his own studio. You can see works from this period in the *Picasso Museum* (see p. 37).

Soon Picasso became part of the vibrant art and bohemian scene of Barcelona. The meeting place was the *Els Quatre Gats* restaurant, which is still in existence today. This is where Picasso had his first exhibition, in 1900 – for which he designed the vignettes on the menu. This was also when he painted *Les Demoiselles d'Avignon*. Don't be misled by the title of this famous painting, though: Picasso drew his inspiration not from the ladies in the southern French town of Avignon, but from those of the red-light district of Barcelona's Old Town, around Carrer Avinyó. In 1904, Picasso moved to Paris for good.

GARDENERS AGAINST LAND GRABS

You might be surprised to come across vegetation and the scent of flowers in the heart of the Old Town, or while heading up to *Park Güell*. Barcelona is home to hordes of keen amateur gardeners, who transform uncultivated plots into blooming community gardens in the blink of an eye.

However, these *Horts Comunitaris* are not just a weekend pastime for sentimental nature-lovers; they are also a protest against real-estate speculation and inflated prices. The idea behind this activism is that wherever beans and tomatoes grow, office buildings cannot. On a few occasions the guerrilla gardeners have even managed to seriously interfere with the plans of ambitious developers – such as in the Old City neighbourhood of Sant Pere. Here, plans were originally in place to build a set of luxury apartments and a multi-storey car park on the Forat de la Vergonya; now, however, there is a children's playground and an organic garden, both painstakingly built and maintained by local residents.

URBAN SUPERBLOCK!

Flowerpots blocking the way of cars? Bright yellow hopscotches painted on the tarmac? Tactical urbanism is the name of the game, because Barcelona wants to drastically reduce the

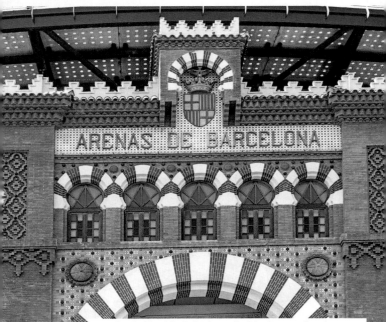

An end to the bloodshed: this former bullring is now a shopping centre

number of cars in its city centre by 2030. The plan is to combine several blocks of houses into so-called "super-blocks". Traffic will be rerouted around the outside, and the former roads will be greened over and transformed into playgrounds and picnic areas for residents. See – and try! – the pilots for yourself in Sant Antoni (see p. 55) and Poblenou.

TAKING THE BULL BY THE HORNS

Traditionally, bullfighting is sacred to the Spanish – the Catalans, however, find it rather suspect: more and more of them are rejecting this centuries-old tradition as cruelty to animals. In 2010, a historic decision was taken in the regional parliament: Catalonia became the first region on the Spanish mainland to ban bullfighting – that is, until the Spanish Constitutional Court judges scrapped the law in 2016. But if they hoped the Catalan community in favour of the *toros* would flourish, they will have been sorely disappointed. In fact, the opposite has happened.

What was once the city's largest bullring has long since become a shopping centre, and work has been under way for years to transform another into a concert hall.

Catalonia, meanwhile, has its own regional tradition of the *correbous*, where the bull is chased through the streets wearing a torch on his horns – and there's no bloody ending.

SIGHT SEEING

Barcelona! The name alone is enough to make anyone's eyes sparkle. And no wonder! Where else do you find so many and varied sights all in one place?

The largest Gothic quarter after the one in Prague; the splendid monuments of *Modernisme*; ultramodern creations by international star architects and designers, from Jean Nouvel to Norman Foster: Barcelona's image has been and still is determined through its art and culture. But you don't need to pay entry fees or stand in line to discover all these creations: art forms a natural part of city life,

You'll find all the venues in this chapter on the pull-out map 📖

Gaudí avoided using any load-bearing walls in his Casa Milà

whether on the streets or *plaças*, in houses, courtyards, parks or patios. So, if you want to get close to the much-vaunted beauty of Barcelona, make sure you have time to just drift.

For many of the more popular tourist attractions, such as Park Güell, Sagrada Família or the Picasso Museum, you can buy tickets online in advance to avoid the long queues. For more information visit the *Palau de la Virreina (Rambla 99 | tel. 933 017 775 | bcn.es/icub)* or check with the tourist board information points *(barcelona turisme.com)*.

CITY OVERVIEW

Park Güell ★

MARCO POLO HIGHLIGHTS

Ronda del General Mitre

EIXAMPLE p. 39

Square, practical and beautiful! Modernisme makes its grand entrance here

Carrer de Balmes

Avinguda de Sarrià

Carrer de París

RAVAL & LA RAMBLA p. 46

Enjoy the promenade in Barcelona's creative melting pot

Gran Via de les Corts Catalanes

Museu Nacional d'Art de Catalunya ★

Munta

Mon

Carrer de Lepant

SANT PERE, SANTA CATERINA & LA RIBERA p. 35

Civic pride meets a long history of craft – plus, plenty of boutiques to browse in between!

Sagrada Família ★

BARRI GÒTIC p. 30

Secluded squares and plush palaces: the Old Town brings the Middle Ages to life

Casa Milà ★

Palau de la Música Catalana ★

Museu Picasso ★

Catedral ★

Barri Gòtic ★

La Rambla ★

Ronda Litoral

BARCELONETA & THE PORTS p. 48

A dip in the sea followed by a seafood feast – the city beach can offer both

Fundació Joan Miró ★

MONTJUÏC & POBLE SEC p. 52

The view? Unbeatable! And the sights… Barcelona plays its ace card on the museum mountain

Mar Mediterrània

800 m
875 yd

BARRI GÒTIC

With its architectural splendour, the ★ Barri Gòtic, known as the "heart of Barcelona", is a testimony to Catalonia's heyday as a Mediterranean power.

Most buildings and monuments date back to the 14th and 15th centuries, when the citizens' wealth led to a construction boom. Only when Barcelona lost its primacy to Castile in the 16th century did the Gothic Quarter start to decline. The historic buildings were restored as part of the Olympic urban redevelopment although to this day many of the residential buildings are still run-down. For some time now the urban developers and architects have had their eye on this old part of town, and in their wake have attracted the usual speculators and property sharks who are pushing the resident population out of their cheap accommodation: old people, students, artists or immigrants. Hip boutiques, chic cafés and trendy bars are opening up alongside the traditional barbers and corner shops. Still, you can gain a lively impression of the Catalans' history and attitude to life in the maze of the old quarter's alleyways and back lanes.

■ PLAÇA DEL REI

A unique architectural ensemble! The *Palau Reial Mayor*, the royal palace, with its large *Saló del Tinell* banquet hall and imposing watchtower, the *Mirador del Rei Martí* (a kind of medieval high-rise), as well as the adjoining *Palau del Lloctinent* (Palace of the Lieutenant, Gothic façade, Renaissance inner courtyard) and the small Gothic chapel of *Santa Agata* (14th century) form a splendid backdrop, especially in the evening sunshine.

The acoustics are also splendid – in the summer, interesting concerts take place here. The *Saló del Tinell* was where the Spanish kings received Columbus after his return from America, and where the Inquisition held court in the 15th century – those condemned as heretics were burned on the square below. The palace interior is reached through the Museum of City History at the other end of the Plaça del Rei. *Metro L4: Jaume I | ▥ c3*

■ MUSEU D'HISTÒRIA DE LA CIUTAT (MUSEUM OF CITY HISTORY) ☎

Take the lift down to the basement and you might feel like you've stepped

Barcelona's La Rambla boulevard is never quiet

into a time machine. Below, you will discover a 4,000m² field of ruins: canals, streets, workshops and mosaic floors give a good impression of life in Roman Barcino. This walk through one of Europe's largest archaeological sites is also great fun for children! The upper floors of the Gothic palace show remains of the Roman city wall as well as exhibits from medieval and modern times. *Tue–Sat 10am–7pm, Sun 10am–8pm | admission 5 euros incl. admission to all other MUHBA museums | Plaça del Rei | barcelona.cat/museuhistoria | metro L4: Jaume I | ⏱ 1 hr | 🗺 c3*

🖪 MUSEU FREDERIC MARÈS

Sculptor Frederic Marès (1893–1991) was a passionate traveller and collector of art. The museum's sculpture section showcases his collection of works from Roman times and the Romanesque, Gothic, Renaissance and Baroque periods. The Collector's Cabinet reveals everyday objects from the 15th to 18th centuries.

Particularly lovely are the rooms dedicated to the worlds of women gone by. Where else could you admire handicrafts lovingly braided from a lock of your sweetheart's hair? *Tue–Sat 10am–7pm, Sun 11am–8pm | admission 4.20 euros; free admission every 1st Sun of the month and every Sun from 3pm | Plaça Sant Iu 5 | barcelona.cat/museufredericmares | metro L4: Jaume I | ⏱ 1 hr | 🗺 c3*

INSIDER TIP
Cabinet of curiosities for romantics

BARRI GÒTIC

Plaça del Rei **1**

Museu Frederic Marès **3**

Catedral ★ 5

Palau Episcopal

2 Museu d'Història de la Ciutat

Via Laietana

Plaça de Sant Felip Neri **4**

Palau de la Generalitat de Catalunya

Carrer de Jaume I

Plaça de Sant Jaume **6**

Carrer de Perrinol

Carrer del Pi

Carrer del Call

Carrer de Canora

Barri Gòtic ★

Palau Centelles

Carrer de Ferran

Carrer de Palau

Carrer d'Ataülf

Carrer d'en Gignàs

Carrer Ample

La Rambla

Carrer d'Avinyó

7 Plaça Reial

Carrer d'en Rull

Carrer dels Còdols

100 m
109 yd

8 Palau Güell

4 PLAÇA DE SANT FELIP NERI

German director Tom Tykwer was so taken with the enchanting atmosphere of this small Old Town square with its baroque church and fountain beneath the acacia trees that he set part of his film *Perfume* here. The idyll now only exists on celluloid. The hordes of tourists has ballooned to such an extent that the city sometimes closes the entrance on weekdays so that the children of the adjacent school can spend their breaktimes in peace on the square. The holes in the church façade are a stark reminder of the bombardments by the Italian air force during the Spanish Civil War. Today, a memorial plaque commemorates the civilians who sadly died, most of them schoolchildren. Antoni Gaudí would often come here on his evening walks while he was working on the Sagrada Família. *Metro L1, L3: Calalunya | □ c3*

5 CATEDRAL (CATHEDRAL) ★

Construction of this imposing church was started in the 11th century on the foundations of an Early Christian basilica destroyed by the Moors. However, it was only between 1298 and 1448 that the magnificent nave was given its current form, while the neo-Gothic main façade was only completed in 1890. The choir stalls in the centre of the church are exquisite – a work by Flanders' native Pere Ça Anglada. One of the 29 side chapels mainly dating from the 16th and 17th centuries holds an allegedly miraculous crucifix. It is said to have helped gain victory against the Turks in the great sea battle of Lepanto. The cathedral is dedicated to the martyr Santa Eulàlia, one the city's two patron saints, who was tortured to death in late Roman times. The saint is buried in an alabaster sarcophagus in the crypt below the high altar.

Also worth seeing is the enchanting cloister with its small chapels, garden, a Gothic fountain and a flock of geese. The 13 geese are a reminder of each year of Saint Eulàlia's life. The cloister gives access to the small museum *(Mon–Sat 1–5pm, Sun 2–5pm | admission 7 euros)* of the cathedral, which shows archaeological finds and Gothic altarpieces. *Mon–Fri 9.30am–6.30pm, Sat 9.30am–5.15pm, Sun 2–5pm | 9 euros (incl. visit to the choir stalls, museum and elevator up the church tower) | Plaça de la Seu | catedralbcn. org | metro L4: Jaume I | ⊙ 1 hr | ▥ c3*

INSIDER TIP
Saintly geese

6 PLAÇA DE SANT JAUME

This square in the Gothic quarter is where Catalan history was made and is still being made today. As far back as 2,000 years ago, when Barcelona was still the Roman settlement of Barcino, this was the hub of municipal life. It was on this square that in 1931 the Catalan republic was proclaimed; from here the president of Catalunya, Josep Tarradellas, returning from exile in 1977, shouted out to the rapturous crowd his legendary sentence: *"Ja sóc aquí"* ("I'm back"). To this day, the Catalans congregate on Plaça de Sant Jaume to demonstrate or party. Architecturally too, the square is remarkable. On one side stands the *Palau de la Generalitat (guided tours every second and fourth weekend of the month Sat/Sun 10am–1.30pm, only with reservation | free | president. cat)*, seat of the autonomous Catalan regional government. The palace was erected between 1403 and 1630

Up and up and up: the nave of the city's Gothic cathedral stretches heavenwards

Beneath the palm trees: summertime on the beautiful Plaça Reial

around a Gothic core. Don't miss the pretty Sant Jordi (St George's) Chapel, the domed Sant Jordi Hall with ceiling paintings and the ornate Golden Hall, reached via the charming Courtyard of Orange Trees.

Opposite lies the *city hall (guided tours every half hour Sun 10am– 1.30pm | free).* The well-preserved Gothic part of the 14th-century Ajuntament with the splendid assembly hall of the *Consell de Cent* (Council of the Hundred) and its magnificent inner courtyard is worth seeing. The city hall's neoclassical façade dates from the 19th century. *Metro L4: Jaume I | ⫿ c3*

7 PLAÇA REIAL

One of the most beautiful squares of the city, the Royal Square dates from 1859. The arcaded complex of neoclassical buildings was erected on top of a former Capuchin monastery. Its centre is occupied by the Three Graces fountain, which was later joined by Modernist lanterns designed by Antoni Gaudí. For a time the square became a run-down shelter for the drug trade and prostitution, but it was renovated entirely and today has terraced cafés, restaurants, jazz clubs and discos. *Metro L3: Liceu | ⫿ b3*

8 PALAU GÜELL

An early work by Antoni Gaudí, which established his reputation as one of the greatest architects and craftsmen of his time, the ornate palace was built in 1889 for his friend and patron Eusebi Güell. The asymmetrical façade and the bizarre chimneys of the roof landscape already presage Gaudí's break with the geometrical forms that still dominated architecture at the time. Don't miss the impressive organ

under the dome! *April–Oct Tue–Sun 10am–7pm; Nov–March 10am–4pm; last admission 1 hr before closing | admission 12 euros incl. audio guide | C/ Nou de la Rambla 3 | palauguell.cat | metro L3: Liceu | ⏲ 1 hr | 🕮 b3*

SANT PERE, SANTA CATERINA & LA RIBERA

Where craftsmen of the 13th and 14th centuries dyed leather, wove cloth, hammered, pottered and carpentered, today's contemporary artists and craftspeople showcase their talents. The shops in the old quarter of Ribera now house studios, bars or boutique shops.

With its narrow archways, tight streets and secluded squares, the quarter, which was renovated in the 1980s, has retained much of its authentic atmosphere. The lively Ribera district, also known as El Born, is only a few paces away from one of the city's most attractive parks, the *Parc de la Ciutadella*.

9 PALAU DE LA MÚSICA CATALANA ★ ⚑

Built by Lluís Domènech i Montaner between 1905 and 1908, this Palace of Music boasts the most unrestrained Art Nouveau style. Towards Carrer Sant Pere Més Alt the façades are opulently adorned, with mosaic-covered columns crowned by the busts of Bach, Beethoven, Wagner and Palestrina. The concave dome of colourful glass in the centre of the auditorium is of extraordinary beauty, while the ceilings, walls and pillars are covered in flowers and tendrils, as well as dragons' heads and other symbolic sculptures. Guided tours even offer visitors the chance to take to the stage themselves – well, for a few minutes! *Guided tours Sept–June daily 10am–3.30pm every 30 mins; July 10am–6pm; Aug 9am–6pm | admission 19 euros | C/Palau de la Música 4–6 | tel. 932 957 200 | palaumusica.org | metro L1, L4: Urquinaona | ⏲ 50 mins | 🕮 c2*

10 PLAÇA DE SANT PERE ⚑

Here, in the late Middle Ages, a small stream powered the area's textile mills; today the area is home to young artists, designers and restaurateurs. But the small square and surrounding streets, around the *Carrer de les Basses de Sant Pere*, haven't lost their medieval charm. Pause for a moment at the former Benedictine convent of *Sant Pere de Puelles* – the perfect spot for some people-watching. Romantics in

INSIDER TIP
Daydream under the trees

particular will feel at home under the leafy roof of Plaça Sant Augustí Vell. The bars around the lantern fountain are perfect for a few tapas or a drink. *Plaça de Sant Pere | metro L1, L4: Urquinaona | ⊞ d2*

⓫ MERCAT DE SANTA CATERINA

The brainchild of Barcelonan architect couple Enric Miralles and Benedetta Tagliabue, the brightly coloured, wavy roof of the market hall has become the district's trademark. The site was once a monastery, which was demolished during the *desamortización* in the mid-19th century, when church property was seized by the Spanish government and sold to secular ownership. The apse of the monastery was rediscovered during reconstruction work. It's worth a visit for the colourful market hustle and bustle alone, which is far more relaxed than in the overcrowded Boqueria. And if you have worked up an appetite, the bars at the back offer authentic treats. *Mon–Sat 7am–4pm | Av. de Francesc Cambó 16 | mercatsantacaterina.com | metro L4: Jaume 1 | ⊞ c3*

⓬ MUSEU EUROPEU D'ART MODERN (MEAM)

At the European Museum of Modern

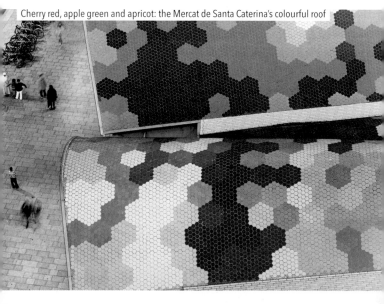

Cherry red, apple green and apricot: the Mercat de Santa Caterina's colourful roof

SANT PERE, SANTA CATERINA & LA RIBERA

10 Plaça de Sant Pere

9 Palau de la Música Catalana ★

11 Mercat de Santa Caterina

Parc de la Ciutadella

El Born Centre Cultural 16 | Parc de la Ciutadella 17

13 Museu Picasso ★

Museu Europeu d'Art Modern (MEAM) 12

14 MOCO Museum Barcelona

Santa Maria del Mar 15

Art you'll find an impressive collection of sculptures as well as photography and painting. The common denominator? Everything shown in the halls of the Renaissance palace, *Palau Gomis*, is figurative and by 20th- and 21st-century European artists. Visit on Fridays and Saturdays when jazz and classical concerts transform a trip into a real-life immersive piece. *Tue–Sun 11am–7pm | admission 11 euros | Barra de Ferro 5 | meam.es | metro L4: Jaume I | ⏲ 1 hr | 🗺 c3*

INSIDER TIP
A feast for the eyes becomes a feast for the ears

13 MUSEU PICASSO (PICASSO MUSEUM) ★

The city's most visited museum mainly shows works from the early creative period of Pablo Picasso – the Blue Period – which coincides with his years in Barcelona. Living in the Catalan metropolis between 1895 and 1904, the painter was part of the artistic avant-garde and bohemian scene and this was where he found first recognition. All his life he felt a strong tie to Barcelona, even during the Franco dictatorship when he was exiled in France. From the 1930s Picasso would donate paintings to the city, amongst them his famous *Harlequin*, but it was only in 1963 that the scattered works were united under one museum roof – on the initiative of Picasso's friend and secretary Jaume Sabartés. Initially housed in a Gothic palais on Carrer de Montcada, the museum today extends across five splendid residences. Bit by bit the collection was completed, Picasso gifting the museum his famous Menina series and all early works from the family's residence in Barcelona; his widow Jacqueline added valuable ceramics. Today, the museum represents the most important public Picasso collection alongside the one in Paris. Be sure to book online in advance and don't miss your time slot! *Tue–Sun 9am–7pm, Thu until 9.30pm | admission 12 euros, children and under 18s free |* 🐷 *Thu 5–8pm and every first Sun of the month free (but you must still reserve tickets) | C/ de Montcada 15–23 | museupicassobcn. cat/en | metro L4: Jaume I | ⓧ 2 hrs | ▥ d3*

Museu Picasso: five palaces full of masterpieces on a Gothic street

🔢 MOCO MUSEUM BARCELONA

Damien Hirst, Jeff Koons and Mark Rothko: this branch of the Amsterdam museum has all the big names in modern and contemporary art – names that fetch the top prices at auctions! The mostly large-scale works are housed in the city palace of the Cervelló family, opposite the Picasso Museum. There isn't much explanatory info, but plenty of shots for "Insta"! *Daily 9am–10pm | admission 14.50 euros | C/ de Montcada 25 | mocomuseum.com | metro L4: Jaume I | ⓧ 1 hr | ▥ d3*

🔢 SANTA MARIA DEL MAR 🛆

For many, this has to be the most beautiful church in Barcelona. Designed in pure Catalan Gothic style, the fascination of this church resides in its artful simplicity: no pomp or circumstance disturbs the impression of space, openness and meditative silence. Skilfully designed polychrome stained-glass windows, partly from the 15th century, bathe the almost empty nave (the choir stalls and furnishings were burned in the Civil War) in near-mystical light. The building with its tall slender columns inside, was erected between 1329 and 1384 – record time for a big medieval church, which also helps to explain its stylistic uniformity. If you have the chance to attend a concert here, you can enjoy the extraordinary acoustics as well as the architecture. 🛆 On weekdays the church is open after and on Sundays before the regular opening

> **INSIDER TIP**
> **Gothic acoustics**

hours when you can visit for free in silence. *Mon–Sat 9am–6pm, Sun 1.30–5pm | admission 5 euros | Plaça de Santa Maria 1 | santamariadel marbarcelona.org | metro L4: Jaume I | ▥ d3*

16 EL BORN CENTRE CULTURAL

The historic market hall stands on the ruins of the city destroyed by the Spanish in 1714. The ruins have been uncovered and the former street pattern is clearly visible from the balustrades. This spot is "Ground Zero" for patriotic Catalans, which is why a Catalan flag over 17m tall waves in front of this cultural and exhibition centre that doubles as a memorial. *Nov–March Tue–Sun 10am–7pm; April–Oct 10am–8pm | building and excavations are free, guided tour 4 euros | C/ del Commerç 2 | elborn centrecultural.bcn.cat | metro L1: Arc de Triomf, L4: Jaume I | ▥ d3*

17 PARC DE LA CIUTADELLA 🛝

Today the park with its lake provides some peace and quiet, in a place where once there stood a citadel detested by the Catalans. Erected in 1715 by Philip V after his victorious siege of Barcelona, the fortification served as a feared prison for the subjugation of the rebellious Catalans who did not rest until the citadel fell in 1878 and a park was established on the grounds. In 1888, the complex was turned into the site for the Universal Exhibition. At the main entrance of the park, a fairy-tale castle-like building with golden crenellations is the former exhibition

restaurant *Castells dels Tres Dragons*, designed by architect Lluís Domènech i Montaner.

At the centre of the park is the tall cascade with its extravagant sculpture, in which Gaudí was involved as a student. 🛝 Children will love the life-size replica of a mammoth with an eminently climbable trunk! At the lower end of the park lies *Barcelona Zoo (Nov–March daily 10am–5pm; March–mid-May and mid-Sept–Oct daily 10am–6pm; mid-May–mid-Sept daily 10am–7pm | admission 21.40 euros, children 3-12 years old 12.95 euros | zoobarcelona.com)*. However, the zoo is gradually downsizing, and many enclosures are empty. Next to it stands the Catalan Parliament, housed in the Citadel's former armoury – one of two remaining buildings. *Park daily 9am until dusk | metro L1: Arc de Triomf, L4: Ciutadella | ▥ K10–11*

EIXAMPLE

What makes the quarter unique are its splendid buildings in Catalan Art Nouveau style. In the Quadrat d'Or, the Golden Square (south of Av. Diagonal, between Aribau and Sant Joan), over 150 buildings have been listed now, and they vie to surpass each other in beauty.

All this glory was born in the 19th century as a residential quarter for the up-and-coming Catalan bourgeoisie to designs by Ildefons Cerdà, a young, progressive construction engineer. Cerdà was thinking of a revolutionary project in the American mould: a modern light-filled town with a generously laid-out grid of streets. His designs, however, were only realised in a rather twisted version, although the magnificent buildings are more than worth a visit. But the Eixample is much more than an Art Nouveau open-air museum: shops, galleries, restaurants, bars and street cafés make it one of the city's most vibrant quarters.

18 PASSEIG DE GRÀCIA

This swanky boulevard boasts magnificent Art Nouveau buildings and palaces, among them important monuments of *Modernisme*, such as Gaudí's La Pedrera and the Casa Milà (see p. 43). To this day, exclusive fashion shops (🐾 check out Massimo Dutti at no. 69), jewellers, luxury hotels and fancy restaurants cluster here – but also increasingly fast-food tapas bars and flagship stores belonging to the big fashion chains. *Metro L2, L3, L4: Passeig de Gràcia | ▥ c1*

19 CASA LLEÓ MORERA

Designed by Lluís Domènech i Montaner (1902–06), this corner house displays decor that has been skilfully worked in pure Art Nouveau style, with an inexhaustible variety of floral elements, whether painted, in stone, plaster, glass, wood or ceramics. The Casa Lleó Morera joins Josep Puig i Cadafalch's Casa Amatller and Gaudí's Casa Batlló to create the fantastical *Mançana de la Discòrdia*, the "houses of discord" or the "apple of discord", in reference to the Greek legend about Paris and the golden apple of discord. In reality, the three stars of *Modernisme* are said to have got along just fine, without a single argument. *The building can currently only be seen from the outside | Passeig de Gràcia 35 | tel. 936 762 733 | casa lleomorera.cat | metro L2, L3, L4: Passeig de Gràcia | ▥ J8*

20 CASA AMATLLER

With its austere stepped gables, this house wouldn't look out of place in the Netherlands – at least at first glance. On closer inspection, however, you can find the playful ornamentation and colours typical of Catalonian Art Deco. The building and its interior were designed by Josep Puig i Cadafalch (one of the three great Catalonian architects alongside Antoni Gaudí and Lluís Domènech i Montaner) for the master chocolatier Antoni Amatller. It was finished off with ultra-modern details like a garage with turntable and an electric food lift. Luckily, the patron had deep pockets to foot the bill thanks to the flourishing chocolate business!

The lovingly packaged chocolate bars with *Modernisme* motifs, as well as the hot chocolate are still popular today, with tastings in the former kitchen. Please note, high heels are not allowed because of the delicate parquet flooring. *Guided 1-hr tours daily 11am (English), 1pm (Spanish); short tours (30 mins) 11.30am, 12.30pm, 3.30pm, 4.30pm, 5.30pm, 6pm | guided tour with chocolate tasting 24 euros, short*

INSIDER TIP
Sightseeing for the sweet-toothed

EIXAMPLE

Hospital de Sant Pau **26**

Sagrada Família ★ **25**

24 Palau Baró de Quadras

23 Casa Milà ★

Plaça de Tetuan

Fundació Antoni Tàpies
22

21 Casa Batlló
20 Casa Amatller
19 Casa Lleó Morera

Passeig de Gràcia **18**

400 m
437 yd

tour 19 euros | Passeig de Gràcia 41 | amatller.com | metro L2, L3, L4: Passeig de Gràcia | ⏱ 1½ hrs | ☐ J8

21 CASA BATLLÓ ⚑

A giant reptile made of stone – with columns that look like elephants' feet, balconies like bones, and a gently undulating façade decorated with glittering mosaics that are reminiscent of colourful scales. While Antoni Gaudí worked on this fantastical house between 1904 and 1907 he had in mind the story of St George the dragon-slayer, who is also the patron saint of Barcelona. The original furniture inside gives a good impression of the life of an upper-middle-class family. Otherwise, everything is pretty high tech: tablet in hand, visitors walk through the seven-floor building, which has been declared a World Heritage Site, and meet holograms of client and architect along the way.

Down in the basement, an immersive installation translates Gaudí's spirit into the design vocabulary of the 21st century. *Daily 9am–8.15pm) | admission from 35 euros (incl. audio guide), children under 12 go free. Watch out: there is an additional 4 euro charge at the ticket office | Passeig de Gràcia 43 | casabatllo.es | metro L2, L3, L4: Passeig de Gràcia | ⏱ 1 hr 15 mins | ▥ J8*

22 FUNDACIÓ ANTONI TÀPIES (TÀPIES FOUNDATION)

In 1990, Antoni Tàpies (1923–2012), one of Catalonia's most important artists, opened his own museum. Built by Art Nouveau architect Lluís Domènech i Montaner, the building houses one of the most comprehensive collections of the works by the *informel* painter and sculptor. There are also changing exhibitions featuring international artists. *Tue–Sun 10am–7pm | admission 8 euros | C/ d'Aragó 255 | fundaciotapies.org | metro L2, L3, L4: Passeig de Gràcia | ⏱ 1 hr | ▥ J8*

23 CASA MILÀ ⭐

Pretty weird: the curved façade on this quirky building looks as if it was moulded from modelling clay, while the columns are reminiscent of gnarled tree trunks. Gaudí's most famous house does not have a single load-bearing wall, and anyone who contemplates Casa Milà is entitled to

Was Gaudí a genius or a freak? Whichever, Casa Milà is a crazy creation

wonder whether its creator was brilliant or insane. He may well have been both! With an underground garage and movable interior walls, the building was once state of the art. At any rate, the local nickname for the building is *La Pedrera*, or "the quarry" – it is completely built out of natural stone.

Those with a head for heights can climb onto the roof: the bizarre roof landscape of chimneys and flues sometimes appear like helmeted soldiers – with a panoramic view thrown in. No wonder the building was declared a UNESCO World Heritage Site. The visit includes one apartment, the roof terrace and the *Espai Gaudí* with multimedia information on the life and work of the master architect. The night-time tours with sparkling wine, video projections and live music on the rooftop terrace are a particular highlight. The illuminations in beautiful Art Deco colours make the building look like a confection, and it is hard to tear your eyes away from it. Best to book online. *March–Oct daily 9am–8.30pm; Nov–Feb daily 9am–6pm | admission 25 euros, night tours March–Oct 9–11pm; Nov–Feb 7–8.40pm, 35 euros, jazz concerts in the summer Fri/Sat | Passeig de Gràcia 92 | lapedrera.com | metro L3, L5: Diagonal | ⏱ 1½ hrs | ⬚ J7*

24 PALAU BARÓ DE QUADRAS

Diagonally opposite the brick building *Cases de Les Punxes* with its six pointed turrets not totally unlike Neuschwanstein Castle in Germany, Modernist genius Josep Puig i Cadafalch built a majestic palace for Manuel Quadras i Feliu. Inside, you can marvel at how the elites of years gone by harnessed the design vocabulary of Gothic and medieval legends. Baron Quadras even had his own coat of arms carved in stone! *Guided tours Fri 10am, 11.15am, 12.30pm (book online) | 15 euros | Av. Diagonal 373 | casessingulars.com | metro L3, L5: Diagonal | ⏱ 1 hr | ⬚ J7*

25 SAGRADA FAMÍLIA ★ ⚑

You don't have to be religious to lose yourself in the front of the Sagrada Família. Outside, the stalactite towers fight for light like trees, and Gaudí's detailed Christmas façade is fascinating. Inside, the sunlight paints an enchanting array of colours on the curved columns and walls. Construction on the massive basilica began in 1882, but Antoni Gaudí would go on to spend four decades of his life on the "Temple of Atonement of the Holy Family", with the last 12 years exclusively dedicated to this project. When he died in 1926, he had only completed the apse, one of the 18 planned towers, the neo-Gothic crypt and the eastern façade dedicated to the Birth of Christ (Christmas façade) – about a tenth of the complete work. Since then, a team of expert architects and computer scientists has been hard at work trying to correctly decipher Gaudí's few surviving directions. If the eternal building site is ever actually finished, it will be crowned with 18 towers. The highest tower will rise 170m into the sky

– higher than any other building, but lower than the "God-made" Montjüic. That said, the second-highest tower, at 13m, dedicated to the Virgin Mary, has since been completed and crowned with a many-pointed star.

Gaudí conceived his mammoth temple as a "sermon in stone", where every detail has a religious meaning: from the 21 birds on the Tree of Life on the Nativity façade, which stand for three (Trinity) times seven (perfection), to the four "evangelist" columns inside, formed from the hardest stone in the world. He also used geometric forms based on mathematical formulae, which successor architects have attempted to reinterpret, although not always with resounding success. The Suffering façade designed posthumously by the sculptor Josep Subirachs, for example, was met with criticism. Opponents condemn the whole project as kitsch and rail against Gaudílandia, the daily circus surrounding the large construction site.

All this has done as little harm to the steady flow of visitors as the fact the Temple of Atonement's patrons include arch-conservative Catholics. It's best to buy your tickets online in advance and watch out for your time slot! 🖐 If you just want to peek inside, you can visit the church on Sundays at 9am for Mass, although seats can be scarce. *April–Sept daily 9am–8pm; Oct and March daily 9am–7pm; Nov–Feb 9am–6pm | admission with audio guide 26 euros, with guided tour (English) 30 euros, with tower 36*

Sagrada Família: Gaudí's unfinished masterpiece attracts many visitors

euros | Plaça de la Sagrada Família | sagradafamilia.org | metro L2, L5: Sagrada Família | ⏱ 2 hrs (with tower tour and crypt) | ⊞ L7

26 HOSPITAL DE SANT PAU

It's no secret that patients recover more quickly in pleasant surroundings – so it's all the more strange that most hospitals are designed as grey concrete bunkers. This hospital, designed in the early 20th century by Domènech i Montaner, is the one exception. In order for the patients to recuperate better in the fresh air and in green spaces, he built 26 individual pavilions covered with colourful ceramic tiles in a park and decorated them with bright mosaics. Corridors and service offices were hidden underground. The visit to one of the world's largest Art Nouveau monuments begins in the former A&E department and leads through underground corridors into the gardens. In the operating theatre guides explain how operations were actually performed in those days, before visitors are directed to the central administration building, complete with its enchanting stained-glass windows and magical domes. The sacred touch is all part of the idea! For good reason: the hospital is diagonally opposite the Sagrada Família. *Daily 10am–6.30pm | admission 16 euros, with audio guide 20 euros | Sant Antoni Maria Claret 167–171 | santpaubarcelona.org | metro L5: Hospital de Sant Pau | ⏱ 1 hr | ⊞ M6*

RAVAL & LA RAMBLA

Raval contrasts clash more visibly than anywhere else in Barcelona: crumbling alleyways rub shoulders with avant-garde boutiques, hip bars and cheap pubs, lounge bars, luxury hotels, demi-monde establishments and historic buildings. There are long-established residents here as well as immigrants, fashion designers, drug dealers, creatives and artists.

It's barely conceivable that up to the mid-18th century, only monasteries, gardens, hospitals and craft workshops existed in Raval. During industrialisation, factories and workers' lodgings sprang up here, until in

Columbus commemorated on La Rambla

the early 20th century the southern part of the quarter became known as the port and red-light district under the name of *Barri Xino*. However, in the 1990s the by-the-hour hotels and brothels had to make way for the modernisation of the quarter. Entire flights of streets were rebuilt, the Boulevard Rambla del Raval in particular, with its trendy bars and restaurants – not to be confused with Barcelona's famous boulevard of La Rambla (which forms the border between Raval and the Gothic quarter).

🔢 LA RAMBLA ★ 🚩

La Rambla (in Catalan: Les Rambles), the 1.2km-long promenade, tiled with wavy tiles, between Plaça de Catalunya and the port, is populated by a colourful maelstrom of people. Under the trees that line the promenade, tourists from cruise ships hunt for that Mediterranean flair. The city dwellers themselves usually only cross the Rambla, to get from the Gothic quarter to Raval or vice versa. Unless, of course, FC Barcelona is celebrating a victory, when cheering and dancing floods the Canaletes fountain at the top of La Rambla. While the Barcelonians have something of a love-hate relationship with their magnificent boulevard, a visit to the Rambla is still a must as it's the hub of the city's history.

Laid out along a dried-up riverbed, La Rambla was actually outside the city walls up until the 18th century. Monasteries and schools stood here. Only in the 19th century did it become a grand boulevard for Barcelona's upwardly mobile bourgeoisie to stroll

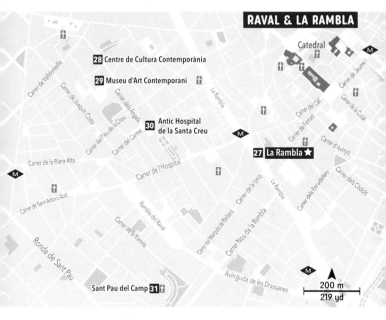

along. And they were happy to line the boulevard with Modernist palaces and an opera house to replace the missing royal court. After a trip to the opera, the gentlemen sometimes headed for the Meublés at the lower end of the Rambla – where small-time criminals and prostitutes still ply their trades today. This promenade is said to mirror the opposing traits that make up the Catalan character: *seny* and *rauxa*. The city administration has been trying for years to bring the chaos of fast-food shops, tourist tat and a few surviving traditional shops into some semblance of order – not entirely without success. At least the famous "living statues" now have a regular spot: in front of the Colombus statue at the port. Metro *L3: Drassanes, Liceu or Catalunya | ◫ b1–4*

⅏ CENTRE DE CULTURA CONTEMPORÀNIA

What does quantum physics have to do with art? How do video games shape our brains? The exhibitions at the Centre for Contemporary Culture can be complex but are always nice to look at. In summer, the courtyard by the foyer is transformed into a stage or open-air cinema. Fancy a break? Why not head for the café on the spacious square inside the building. The view of Keith Haring's graffiti wall is free! *Tue–Sun 11am–8pm | admission 6 euros,* ☛ *Sun from 3pm free of charge | Montalegre 5 | cccb.org | metro L1, L2: Universitat | ⏱ 1½ hrs | ◫ b2*

⅏ MUSEU D'ART CONTEMPORANI

Bright white and flooded with light, elegant and Mediterranean: the avant-garde building (1995) of the Museum of Contemporary Art was designed by star US architect Richard Meier and was the urban prelude to the redevelopment of Raval. The museum shows interesting changing exhibitions on contemporary art, while skaters showcase their contemporary skills on the ramps outside the entrance. If you only get halfway round the museum, you can come back. Tickets are valid for a whole month. *Mon–Fri 11am–7.30pm, Sat 10am–8pm, Sun 10am–3pm | admission 11 euros | Plaça dels Àngels 1 | macba.cat | metro L1, L2: Universitat | ⏱ 1½ hrs | ⌂ b2*

🗑 ANTIC HOSPITAL DE LA SANTA CREU

This unique Gothic hospital complex, once one of the largest in existence, was begun in 1401 and was in operation up to 1926; Antoni Gaudí died in one of the halls here. Barcelona's famous architect had been hit by a tram and was dressed so scruffily that he was mistaken for a beggar and delivered to this hospital for the poor. Today, the building shelters, among other things, the Biblioteca de Catalunya (not open to the public). Make sure you see the romantic inner courtyard complete with orange trees and splashing fountain. In the summer, the library administration digs out a giant chess set, puts out tables and chairs and lays out newspapers and books: a metropolitan oasis, and totally free! *C/ del Carme 47 | metro L3: Liceu | ⌂ b2*

INSIDER TIP
Take a break between monastery walls

🗑 SANT PAU DEL CAMP

The pretty little monastic ensemble on the edge of the *Barri Xino* was built in the 10th century on a green field and is now one of the few remaining Romanesque buildings in Barcelona – an oasis of calm amidst the big-city noise and bustle. *Tue, Thu and Sat 11am–1.30pm and 4.30–6.30pm | admission 5 euros | C/ de Sant Pau 101 | stpaudelcamp.blogspot.com | metro L3: Parallel | ⌂ a3*

BARCELONETA & THE PORTS

This district of Barceloneta became famous as Barcelona's fishing village. With its narrow alleys and lines of washing extending between the houses, there are echoes of the old quarter of Naples. Restaurants now line the promenade of the Old Port, and the beach extends for 4.5km.

On the shores of the Mediterranean, Barceloneta was established in 1753 according to strict rationalist criteria; fishermen, mariners and port workers used to live here in single-storey houses along dead-straight streets. The area grew rapidly, as did the buildings, which were later split into apartments, making Barceloneta one of the most densely populated barrios.

In the course of the Olympic renewal, the Old Port between Barceloneta and La Rambla was turned into a marina and promenade

BARCELONETA & THE PORTS

Parc de la Ciutadella

Olympic Port **35**

Carrer de Sant Pere Més Alt

Carrer de Comerç

Passeig de Picasso

Via Laietana

Passeig de Circumval·lació

Passeig del Doctor Aiguader

Carrer del Gas

Carrer de Balboa

Pla de Palau

Parc de la Barceloneta

Carrer de Ferran

Carrer d'Avinyó

Passeig Marítim de la Barceloneta

Passeig de Colom

Carrer Ample

Carrer d'En Carabassa

Passeig de Joan de Borbó

Mar Mediterrània

La Rambla

Beach **35**

Museu Marítim
32

34 Aquàrium

33 Monument a Cristóbal Colom

400 m
437 yd

lined with restaurants and the beach was given a facelift. Now, the old warehouse at *Moll de la Fusta* houses high-tech start-ups and the *Museu d'Història de Catalunya (Museum of Catalan History) (Tue and Thu–Sat 10am–7pm, Wed 10am–8pm, Sun 10am–2.30pm | admission 6 euros, free on the 1st Sun of the month between 10am and 2.30pm | Plaça de Pau Vila 3 | mhcat.cat).*

Drift through the narrow streets of the Barceloneta fishing district and follow your ears and nose. While rising house prices are increasingly driving long-established tenants out of their once cheap rental flats, you can still find some authentic bars around the marketplace – with excellent fresh fish and a cheerful ambience. From the cablecar *Transbordador del Port*, that takes you up from the pier at the old harbour of Barceloneta to the *Montjuïc*, you have a breathtaking view of the whole city.

32 MUSEU MARÍTIM ☂

Once upon a time, Barcelona was one of the most important seafaring and port cities and the seat of the Crown of Aragon, who ruled much of the western Mediterranean. This gigantic shipyard memorialises this history and is one of the best-preserved and largest of its kind in Europe. Inside, multimedia installations tell the story of Barcelona's maritime past. A real must-see is the painstakingly faithful replica of the *Real Galley*, commanded by Don Juan de Austria for his defeat of the Ottomans in the naval battle of Lepanto.

INSIDER TIP
When land-lubbers set sail

Tempted to turn pirate? The *Santa Eulàlia* is anchored in the Old Port, and entrance is included in the admission to the Museu Marítim *(summer Tue–Fri, Sun 10am–8pm, Sat 2–8pm; winter Tue–Fri, Sun 10am–5.30pm, Sat 2–5.30pm | 3 euros without museum visit).* The fore-and-aft schooner crossed the Atlantic twice in the 1920s. *Av. de les Drassanes | Daily 10am–8pm | admission 10 euros* ☛ *Sun free from 3pm | mmb.cat | tel. 933 429 920 | metro L3: Drassanes |* ⏱ *2 hrs | ⎙ a–b4*

33 MONUMENT A CRISTÓBAL COLOM (COLUMBUS MONUMENT)

When Columbus returned from America in 1493, it was to a ceremonial reception in the port of Barcelona. The 60-m monumental column in the Corinthian style was erected in 1888 for the World Exhibition. The view through the embrasure window is limited, so there is no dramatic panorama and, unless you want the adrenaline rush, a visit from below is more than enough. *Daily 8.30am–2pm | admission 6 euros, online 4 euros at visitbarcelona.com | Plaça del Portal de la Pau | metro L3: Drassanes | ⎙ b4*

Amble safely past sharks: there's no danger in the see-through tunnel of the Aquàrium

34 AQUÀRIUM 👶 🎭

This is one of the largest aquariums in Europe, with over 8,000 animals and plants from all the world's oceans, including replica coral reefs, habitats and deep-sea scenarios. The main attraction is a transparent tunnel over 80m long through which visitors pass below the oceanarium. *Winter daily 10am–7.30pm; summer 10am–8.30 /9.30pm | admission 24 euros, children (aged 3+) 10 euros, and children (aged 5-11) 17 euros | Moll d'Espanya del Port Vell | aquariumbcn.com | metro L4: Barceloneta | ⏱ 2½ hrs | 🗺 J11*

35 OLYMPIC PORT & BEACH 🎭

The urban renewal for the Olympic Games of 1992 opened Barcelona up towards the sea. Where before, a train used to run, there is now a beach 4.5km long. It extends northwards from the old fishermens' quarter Barceloneta to the Olympic village *(Vila Olímpica)* with its modern marina, the *Port Olímpic*, where there's a restaurant, nightclub and pub mile. Also here is Frank O Gehry's 50m-long bronze fish sculpture whose scales shimmering in the sunlight make a great sight. Together with the "twin towers", the Arts luxury hotel and an award-winning office tower, the fish is an Olympics landmark. The beach is also a bonus for children, who can climb, play volleyball, swim or make castles in the sand.

If you walk along the palm-lined beach promenade towards Barceloneta you will end up in the *Parc de la Barceloneta*. The beautiful Art Deco water tower in the middle of the park has a tragic history: the pump mechanism failed during the official opening, and as a result the engineer threw himself from the top floor of the building. A few days later, workers noticed that the English-made key lever had simply been turned in the wrong direction when it was opened!

The hungry and thirsty will be pleased to see 🚩 *Xiringuitos* all along the promenade. From relaxed and beachy to sophisticated elegance, with tapas and drinks to suit all tastes. But watch out! Prices are higher than they are in the neighbourhood proper. *Metro L4: Barceloneta | 🗺 L–Q11*

MONTJUÏC & POBLE SEC

No one gets bored on Montjuïc, Barcelona's 173m-high hill, home to a selection of diverse museums and topped off with a fabulous view of the sea and the city. Once you've seen enough, you can enjoy the refreshing breeze in one of the beautiful parks. And if your stomach is rumbling, head for Poble Sec, the vibrant quarter at the foot of the hill, and Carrer Blai, which is lined with tapas bars.

Montjuïc was first developed for the 1929 World Exhibition, with a few prestigious buildings added during the Olympic Games of 1992. Yet despite all the impressive urban planning, the Barcelonians long nursed rather ambivalent feelings towards their local mountain. But don't forget there's a fortress high up on the mountain, whose cannons were trained on the city several times when the Castilians laid siege to the city. And then, during the Franco dictatorship, the fortification was a feared prison. But, in fact, Barcelona owes its existence to Montjuïc – quite literally: the stones used to build the palaces of the Old Town almost all came from the quarry near the port.

36 FONT MÀGICA

Have you ever applauded a jet of water? No? Well, there's a first time for everything. The Magic Fountain has been thrilling audiences since the 1929 World Exhibition. Several evenings a week, a total of 3,600 nozzles bring the fountains to life, while 120 prismatic spotlights in every colour of the rainbow complete the effect. Totally kitsch? Well, of course! But that's exactly what makes it so great! Why not bring a picnic blanket, bottle of cava and so on and secure a spot at the edge under the tree? *June–Sept Wed–Sun 9.30–10.30pm; 1–10 Oct Thu–Sat 9–10pm; 22 Dec–late March Thu–Sat 8–9pm | Plaça Carles Buïgas 1 | barcelona.cat | metro L1, L3: Espanya | 🗺 E9*

INSIDER TIP
Fountain show? I'll cheer to that!

37 CAIXA FORUM

Interested in contemporary art? The La Caixa foundation possesses one of Europe's most important collections, but it's mostly known for its thoughtful temporary exhibitions. From the life's works of Joseph Beuys to Joan Miró or fashion designer Jean Paul Gaultier: nothing is too much for the makers. The foundation is housed in the spectacularly restored Casaramona, a former textile factory. The imposing Art Nouveau brick building resembling a medieval castle has been fitted with a glass and steel roof. Plus, they put on great concerts and 😀 cinema events for kids. *Daily 10am–8pm | admission 4–6 euros | Av. Marquès de Comillas 6–8 | caixaforum.es | metro L1, L3: Espanya | ⏱ 1½ hrs | 🗺 E9*

38 PAVELLÓ MIES VAN DER ROHE

If you're starting to get tired of the wild forms and colours of *Modernisme*,

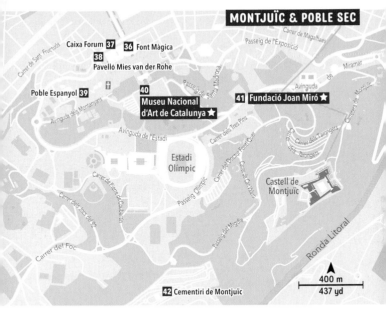

MONTJUÏC & POBLE SEC

Caixa Forum **37** **36** Font Màgica
38
Pavelló Mies van der Rohe
Poble Espanyol **39**
40
Museu Nacional d'Art de Catalunya ★
41 **Fundació Joan Miró** ★
Estadi Olímpic
Castell de Montjuïc
400 m
437 yd
42 Cementiri de Montjuïc

take a break and relax your eyes and senses here. This reproduction of the German pavilion designed by Mies van der Rohe for the 1929 World Exhibition is pretty much the antithesis of the Catalan Art Nouveau of the Caixa Forum directly opposite. With its clean forms, the light marble-and-glass pavilion is a modern icon. *March–Oct 10am–8pm; Nov–Feb 10am–6pm | admission 8 euros | Av. Francesc Ferrer i Guàrdia 7 | miesbcn. com | metro L1, L3: Espanya | ⏱ 45 mins | ▢ E9*

39 POBLE ESPANYOL 😀

The "Spanish village" was intended to give visitors to the 1929 World Exhibition a glimpse of the vast diversity of Spanish architecture in the smallest of spaces. This was completed in painstaking replicas true to the original. In just a few steps, you can walk from Santiago de Compostela to Mallorca or from Besalú in Catalonia to Córdoba in Andalusia. During the day, many of the village's 117 buildings are home, or work, to craftsmen demonstrating their skills, while of an evening, the Poble Espanyol becomes an area for entertainment with restaurants, taverns and clubs. 🐖 Book online to save a few euros, for example on the family package. *Mon 10am–8pm, Tue–Sun 10am–midnight | admission 10 euros for children (aged 4–12) (or 9 euros online), adults 14 euros (online 11.20) | Av. Francesc Ferrer i Guàrdia 13 | pobleespanyol.com | metro L1, L3: Espanya, then bus no. 150 | ⏱ 2 hrs | ▢ E9*

40 MUSEU NACIONAL D'ART DE CATALUNYA (MUSEUM OF CATALAN ART) ★ 🌂 🍴

Find all of Catalonia's art, 2,000 years of it to be exact, under one roof – that of the monumental domed building that was once the exhibition hall at the 1929 World Exhibition and is now the Palau Nacional. And nothing is done by halves here! The collection of Romanesque art is considered unique in the world. Highlights are the colourful Romanesque frescoes. Taken from churches and chapels in the Catalan Pyrenees threatened with collapse, they are today presented in true-to-original replicated apses and altar niches – which brings out the simple beauty of these masterpieces even better. The collection of Gothic art is impressive too. Last but not least you can enjoy exhibits from Renaissance and Baroque times, works by the Catalan Modernists of the late 19th and early 20th century, or modern and contemporary art. Also on display is part of the private Thyssen-Bornemisza collection, providing a unique overview of European art from the Middle Ages to Venetian Late Baroque. Make sure you stop for a moment on the terrace in front of the majestic staircase: the city skyline somehow manages to compete with the works of art inside! *Oct–April Tue–Sat 10am–6pm, Sun 10am–3pm; May–Sept Tue–Sat 10am–8pm, Sun 10am–3pm | admission 12 euros (valid for 2 days within 1 month),* 🐂 *on the 1st Sun of the month and Sat from 3pm free | Palau Nacional | museunacional.cat | metro L1, L3: Espanya | ⏱ 2½ hrs | ⧉ E10*

41 FUNDACIÓ JOAN MIRÓ (JOAN MIRÓ FOUNDATION) ★

The artist himself set up the foundation in 1975. His friend Josep Lluís Sert, one of the leading Spanish

Fundació Joan Miró: Catalan art in the beautiful museum on Montjuïc

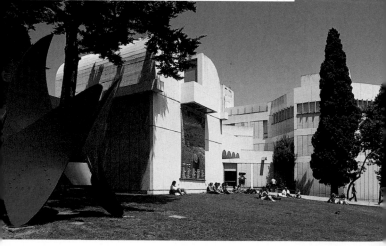

architects of modern times, designed the beautiful museum on the Montjuïc. An open, light-filled, very Mediterranean construction with patios and terraces in harmonious relation to the landscape provides the ideal framework for bringing out the beauty of works by Joan Miró (1893–1983). Get an overview of the creative trajectory of the great Catalan avant-garde painter, who became one of the most famous artists of the 20th century: from his first drawings in 1901 to his very last monumental paintings. The gigantic permanent collection also displays graphic art, wall hangings, ceramics and sculptures, plus changing exhibitions of modern and contemporary art. The bookshop and cafeteria are also recommended! *Sun 10am–6pm all year round; April–Oct Tue–Sat 10am–8pm; Nov–March Tue–Sat 10am–6pm | admission 13 euros | Parc de Montjuïc | fundaciomiro-bcn. org | metro L2, L3: Parallel, then by funicular to Montjuïc | metro L1, L3: Espanya | bus no. 150 | ⊙ 2 hrs | ⌂ F10*

42 CEMENTIRI MONTJUÏC (MONTJUÏC CEMETERY)

A stroll across Barcelona's most beautiful cemetery is like a voyage into the history of the city and its inhabitants. High above the city, the similarly rising bourgeoisie of the 19th century made themselves an ostentatious monument filled with magnificent pantheons and ornate chapels. Prominent artists such as Barcelona-born painter Joan Miró found their last resting place on Montjuïc. *Daily 8am–6pm | C/ de la Mare de Déu de Port 56–58 | cbsa.es | metro L2, L3: Parallel, onwards with bus no. 21, stop: Puig Cementiri del Sud-Oest | ⌂ C–D11*

OTHER SIGHTS

43 SANT ANTONI

You'll struggle to find a true Barcelonian native who hasn't spent at least one Sunday of their childhood in Sant Antoni. The former small-town district between hip Raval and dignified Eixample is known city-wide for its famous flea market specialising in books and comics 🐟 🎭 *Mercat Dominical de San Antoni (Sun 8.30am–2.30pm | Carrer Comte d'Urgell/Carrer Tamarit | dominicaldesantantoni.com)* in front of the market hall, complete with bartering point: on the corner C/ del Comte d'Urgell and C/ Tamarit, fans of scrapbooks and collector's albums have been meeting for decades and swapping their colourful treasures. Come midweek and you can see inside the impressive Modernist market hall *Mercat de Sant Antoni (C/ del Comte Urgell 1 | mercatdesant antoni.com)*. The cruciform brick-and-iron complex by Antoni Rovira i Trias has been lavishly renovated, and part of the old city wall has been uncovered in the basement.

Edge closer towards the sea to admire the *Sant Antoni Superblock*, a masterpiece of urban planning. The junction of C/ Parlament with C/ Comte Borrell has been largely pedestrianised and is now a playground and picnic area for residents, with more blocks to follow!

Fans of a good night out enjoy the vermouth bars on Carrer Parlament.

> **INSIDER TIP**
> **From old-fashioned drink to no. 1 hip tipple**

Long mocked as the Sunday aperitif of greying gentlemen, the slightly bitter vermouth is now celebrating a revival! *Bar Calders (Mon–Fri from 5pm, Sat/Sun from 11pm | Carrer Parlament 25 | tel. 933 299 349 | metro L2: Sant Antoni)* serves the sweet, spiced wine with olive, ice and a slice of orange. *Metro L2: Sant Antoni | ⏷ F–G 9–10*

Jean Nouvel's giant cigar, the colourful Torre Glòries, is a skyline landmark

44 MUSEU DEL DISSENY

What is it that gives design made in Barcelona that certain je-ne-sais-quoi? Discover the answers in this unusual building that juts unabashedly out over Plaça Glòries. Individual exhibitions are devoted to fashion, typography, and product and furniture design. At the end of the day, sit back and relax in one of the sun loungers on the forecourt or stroll across the vast green that is being created on the city's former transport hub. *Tue–Sun 10am–8pm | admission 6 euros, free Sun from 3pm and every first Sun of the month | Plaça de les Glòries Catalanes 37 | museudeldisseny.cat | metro L1: Glóries | ⏱ 1½ hrs | ⏷ M9*

45 TORRE GLÒRIES

Jean Nouvel's cigar-shaped tower, also known as Torre Agbar, has long been one of the city's architectural landmarks with its colourful glass-and-metal façade. Not only do the top floors grant an incredible 360-degree view of the sea of buildings from a height of 125m, but, if you are 12 years or older, you can also clamber through *Cloud Cities Barcelona*, a walk-through sculpture by artist Tomás Saraceno.

> **INSIDER TIP**
> **Spiderman in Barcelona**

Semi-transparent polyhedrons, 113 of them, hang in a kind of gigantic three-dimensional spider's web made of 6km of wire rope! Watch out, though: it takes some skill to clamber through the structure and you should avoid it if you suffer from giddiness. The unusual viewing platform is rounded off by a mirador to

OTHER SIGHTS

Parc del Laberint **50**

Nou Barris

Serra de Collserola

Sant Andreu

Horta
Guinardó **Barcelona**

Tibidabo **51**

Sant Martí

52
Torre de Collserola

CosmoCaixa
Barcelona
53

49 Park Güell ★

Museu Blau **46**

54 Torre Bellesguard

Gràcia

Sarrià Casa Vicens **47 48** Gràcia
Sant Gervasi

45 Torre Glòries
44 Museu del Disseny

Avinguda Diagonal

55 Museu-Monestir Pedralbes

Eixample

Avinguda Diagonal

Les Corts

Ciutat Vella

2 km
1.24 mi

43 Sant Antoni

Sants-Montjuïc

---

the invisible Barcelona in the basement, where data on water, air and noise are processed into projections in real time. *April–Oct daily 10am–9pm; Nov–March daily 10am–7pm | admission 15 euros, incl. Cloud Cities 25 euros | Av. Diagonal 211 | miradortorre glories.com | metro L1: Glòries | ⏱ 1½ hrs | ▥ M9*

46 MUSEU BLAU 🗯

Listen to the rumble of the Earth. Travel back through a time tunnel to the Big Bang. Understand how complex mammals evolved from microbes. Housed in a rather unusual triangular building designed by architectural studio Herzog & de Meuron, the Museum of Natural Sciences explains the history of the earth in vivid detail with skilful staging. Absolutely fascinating is the huge collection of stuffed animals from the city's collection. 🐖 To save some cash, visit the museum on Sundays from 3pm or on the first Sunday of the month. If you want to check out the botanical garden on Montjüic, too, then book the combination ticket for just one euro extra. The spacious square out front is a popular venue for concerts and is something special for sports fans and skaters with its climbing park, sea swimming pool, gigantic sun awning and huge tarmacked zone. *Oct–Feb Tue–Fri 10am–6pm, Sat 10am–7pm, Sun 10am–8pm; March–Sept Tue–Sat 10am–7pm, Sun 10am–8pm | admission 6 euros, children 2.70 euros (free on Sun from 3pm and on the 1st Sun of the month | Plaça Leonardo da Vinci 4–5 |*

museuciencies.cat | metro L4: El
Maresme-Forum | ⏱ 2 hrs | ⎙ Q10–11

⁴⁷ CASA VICENS 🛈

Built between 1883 and 1885, this
upper-middle-class villa was Gaudí's
first major work. While inspired by the
Arab-Spanish Mudéjar style, it already
has that distinct Gaudiesque character.
A single look at the lush bay windows
and the leaves, flowers and little birds
that adorn the walls and ceilings is
enough to tell you that. Opened as a
museum in 2017, the building's second floor houses an exhibition that
aims to delve deep into the thinking
of the Modernist star. *April-Oct daily
10am–8pm; Nov–March Mon 10am–
3pm, Tue–Sun 10am–5pm | admission
18 euros | Carrer de les Carolines
20–26 | casavicens.org | metro L3:
Lesseps |* ⏱ *1 hr | Gràcia |* ⎙ *J5*

⁴⁸ GRÀCIA

This cosy part of town beyond Diagonal
and Passeig de Gràcia has much
neighbourhood feeling. You'll still feel
a bit of the tranquillity of the village
that Gràcia used to be before its incor-
poration into Big Barcelona: small
houses and craft workshops, little bars
and restaurants, corner shops and
street cafés, squares, patios and terraces wherever you go. Don't be
surprised to see donation boxes or fly-
ers at the till: getting behind a good
cause is as much a part of Gràcia as the
organic or Fairtrade logos. Amongst
the most beautiful squares of the district are ⚑ *Plaça de la Vila* and *Plaça de
la Virreina*. In the 1970s, Barcelona's
alternative arts movement started

from Gràcia. Today still, many small
theatres, hip restaurants and bars, galleries and alternative
shops remain. Release
your inner hippy and
let your alternative
soul relax on the Plaça del Sol among
the ever-chill Graciencos. Of an
evening, the square will be filled with
the sound of guitars being plucked…
and maybe the smell of an odd joint.
Metro L3: Fontana, FGC (train): Gràcia |
⎙ *J–K 5–7*

⁴⁹ PARK GÜELL ⭐

Fairy-tale houses, dragon figures,
gigantic grottoes: the picturesque
park laid out above the city by Antoni
Gaudí between 1900 and 1911), was
placed under UNESCO World Heritage
protection. Gaudí's innovative work,
which delighted Salvador Dalí, was a
commission by his patron Eusebi
Güell. The original plan was for a
spacious garden estate; however, only
three houses were built as the budget
ran out!

At the park's centre, a huge terrace
is supported by Doric columns with a
breathtaking panoramic view, rivalled
only by the *Turó de la Rovira*, 100m
above Park Güell. A long curvy stone
bench snakes its way across the terrace made of colourful mosaics from
glass and pottery shards. At the
entrance to the staircase is the lumi-
nous dragon Python, who, according
to legend, guards the subterranean
waters.

The park is a unique, happy combi-
nation of architecture and nature.
Gaudí took care to be economical and

ecological in his constructions, using materials found in the grounds. For his mosaics he used what the neighbouring ceramics factories were throwing away: if you look carefully at the ceiling rosettes, you can make out the undersides of plates or cup handles. And through the inside of the Doric columns rainwater flows into the underground reservoir. Visits are limited, so make sure to book online and allow enough time to get there because the time slots are scheduled to the minute.

For a view from above, the undeveloped part of the park can be visited free of charge, and closes at 11pm – but be warned: there is no lighting of any kind! Only the 12-hectare *Monumental Zone* charges for admission, but this is where you'll snap those most iconic photos! The grounds also hold the *Gaudí Museum (Oct–March 10am–6pm; April–Sept 9am–8pm | admission 5.50 euros | casamuseugaudi.org/en | ⏱ 45 mins)*

in the master's former residence, with mementoes of his life. The interactive Gaudí exhibition *Gaudí Experiencia (Sept–March 10am–5pm; April–Oct 10am–8pm | admission 9 euros | Larrard 41 | gaudiexperiencia.com)* in 4-D is close by with models of never-realised buildings such as a New York skyscraper. *April–Sept 9.30am–7.30pm; Oct–Feb 9.30am–5.30pm; March 9.30am–6pm (time slots outside official opening hours are reserved for Barcelona residents) | admission 10 euros, with guided tour (in English) 22 euros | C/ d'Olot | park guell.barcelona | metro L3: Lesseps (longer, with a steep walk) | bus no. 24: Park Güell (right to the park) | ▢ K4*

🔟 PARC DEL LABERINT

Spring has sprung! The neoclassical gardens are a late 18th- century masterpiece capable of turning the most cynical of visitors into hopelessly romantic teenagers. Time and again you will be surprised by playful Amor

The Casa Vicens is *almost* austere and geometric – well, for a Gaudí building at least

Head for heights? Then hop aboard the Ferris wheel with its incredible views over the city

statues, waterfalls, bridges, fountains and lakes, as well as small marble temples – a loved-up ensemble designed by the Marquis von Alfarràs. Why not whisk your sweetheart away to get gently lost in the maze of cypress hedges? *March/Oct daily 10am-7pm; April 10am-8pm; May-Sept 10am-9pm; Nov-Feb 10am-6pm | admission 2.23 euros, Sun free | metro L3: Mundet | ⌁ N1*

INSIDER TIP
Labyrinth for lovers

51 TIBIDABO 🌂

At 500m this is the city's highest point. The trip up in the open tram carriages of *Tramvia Blau (from Av. del Tibidabo | currently out of service for maintenance, replacement bus no. 196 | 5.50 euros | barcelonabusturistic.cat)* through Barcelona's fancy quarter is quite an experience. At the final stop panorama bars and a garden restaurant await, while a funicular can take you all the way up to the summit, where there's a funfair with Ferris wheel and carousels, as well as the TV tower (see below). *July/Aug Wed–Sun; Sept-Dec and March-June mostly weekends only | admission to fun park free for under 90cm tall, 14 euros for those under 1.20m, and 35 euros for adults and those taller | tel. 932 117 942 | tibidabo.cat | FGC (train): Tibidabo, then Tramvía Blau and funicular or bus no.196 | ⌁ c9*

52 TORRE DE COLLSEROLA (TV TOWER)

Erected for the 1992 Olympic Games, the TV tower on the Tibidabo is the work of famous British architect Sir Norman Foster. From up here you have a fabulous 360-degree view (on a clear day for over 70km) beyond the city. A glass elevator whisks you up at breathtaking speed to the viewing platform at a height of 115m. *Varying opening times, sometimes only open at weekends, see website | admission 5.60 euros | torredecollserola.com | FGC (train): S1, S2 Peu de Funicular, then Funicular Vallvidrera cable car | ▥ G1*

🟥 COSMOCAIXA BARCELONA (SCIENCE MUSEUM) 🎏 🎎

Have you ever looked a crocodile in the eye? You can do it without any risk in the replicated Amazon jungle. At the interactive Science Museum, science and nature are not only explained, but also experienced by experimenting and using your senses. It's great fun! In the *Toca Toca!* area children are welcome to touch the plants and animals along with their habitats. *Daily 10am–8pm | admission 6 euros, free for under 16s, free on the first Sun of the month, extra activities not included in the price | C/ Isaac Newton 26| fundacio.lacaixa.es | bus no. H2, H4, V15, V17, V19 or take L7 to Av. Tibidabo, then Tramvía Blau or walk | ⏱ 1½ hrs | ▥ H3*

🟥 TORRE BELLESGUARD

With its tower, battlements, arrow-slit windows and grey slate walls, you'd be forgiven for thinking this building was a Medieval castle or the set for a Harry Potter film – but you'd be wrong. It was designed by the brilliant Antoni Gaudí and was built in 1902 on the site of the summer residence of the last Catalan king, in homage to Catalonia's Gothic golden age. For nine years Gaudí worked on this house high above the city, and ultimately brought his client's family to the point of bankruptcy. Unlike the austere façade, the interior is bright and flooded with light – with glowing white walls, colourful mosaics and wall tiles. The wonderful panoramic views over Barcelona are enshrined in the villa's name: Bellesguard means "beautiful view". But the view is not the only surprise up on the roof: Gaudí also managed to hide some of his beloved winged monsters in the corners. *Tue–Sun 10am-3pm | admission 9 euro (includes audio guide), guided tours 16 euros | bellesguardgaudi.com | FGC (train): Av. Tibidabo, on by bus 196 to Bellesguard or on the Blue Route of the Bus Turistic | ⏱ 1 hr | ▥ H3*

INSIDER TIP
A dragon's eye view

🟥 MUSEU MONESTIR PEDRALBES

This monastic complex is a gem of Gothic architecture. Inside you'll find medieval furniture, paintings and sculptures. The enchanting two-storey cloister is adorned with 14th-century wall paintings. *Oct–March Tue–Fri 10am–2pm, Sat/Sun 10am–5pm; April–Sept Tue–Fri 10am–5pm, Sat 10am–7pm, Sun 10am–8pm | admission 5 euros, free 1st Sun of the month and every Sun from 3pm | Baixada Monestir 9 | monestir pedralbes.barcelona | FGC (train): Reina Elisenda | ▥ E3*

Surrealism at its best: huge artwork at Teatre-Museu Dalí

AROUND BARCELONA

56 CRIPTA DE LA COLONIA GÜELL

Approx. 20 mins by train (FGC: S3, S4, S7) from Plaça Espanya to Colónia Güell

Only the crypt of the planned church is visible. Nevertheless, it is one of Antoni Gaudí's masterpieces; In fact, many consider the fantastical and complex crypt, which has hardly any right angles, to be his most daring and modern project. The incomplete church stands at the centre of the Modernist workers' colony and factory complex Colonia Güell, founded by textile magnate Eusebi Güell. The site was purposefully located far from the city to "protect" his workers from revolutionary ideas. *Daily 10am–3pm | admission 9.50 euros | Santa Coloma de Cervelló | gaudicoloniaguell.org | ⊞ c9*

57 SITGES

Approx. 30 mins by train (R2S) from Barcelona-Sants

The ideal destination for a day trip to the coast, with kilometres of sandy beaches, palm-lined promenades, museums, bars, cafés, restaurants, boutiques and attractive Art Deco villas all emanating a slightly decadent 19th-century charm, from the days when Sitges was an artists' colony. Today, this lively bathing resort is also a major destination for the international gay community. *By car along the A16 | ⊞ b10*

58 TEATRE-MUSEU DALÍ

55 mins by train (AVE) from Barcelona-Sants to Figueres Vilafant

With enormous white eggs on the roof, bright red walls dotted with

– the fantastic natural backdrop making up for the touristy infrastructure of restaurants and souvenir shops. Don't miss the Gregorian chants intoned at lunchtime by 50 choirboys *(Mon–Fri 1pm, Sun noon). Monastery daily 8am–8pm; winter 9am–5.45pm. Black Madonna 8–10.30am and noon–6.30pm, July–Sept also 7.30–8.10pm | free admission | montserratvisita.com | motorway A2, exit Martorell, then national road NII (approx. 60km north-west of Barcelona) |* ▥ *b9*

⑥⓪ MONESTIR DE POBLET

130km by car on the A2 (exit: Montblanc)

As if the church with its alabaster altar weren't big enough, the impregnable 800-year-old fortifications here also conceal an entire monastic town. This extremely well-preserved Cistercian monastery located about 130km from Barcelona is still home to around 30 monks, who enjoy all mod cons – including solar panels and internet access. Anyone who wants to disconnect and listen to some Gregorian chant is welcome to visit the monastery's modern guesthouse. Make sure you check out the stunning cloister too! *Mid-Sept–mid-March Mon–Sat 10am–12.30pm and 3–6.30pm, Sun 10.30am–12.25pm and 3–6pm; mid-March–mid-Sept Mon–Sat 10am–12.30pm and 3–6pm, Sun 10.30–12.25pm and 3–6pm | admission 8.50 euros, guided tours 10 euros | poblet. cat | train from Sants railway station in the direction of Lleida to L'Espluga de Francoli (approx. 4km from the monastery) |* ▥ *a9*

loaves of bread, and the artist himself embalmed beneath a huge Plexiglas cupola, the Teatre-Museu in Figueres is Dalí's quirky memorial to his own work. Embark on a voyage into the eccentric artist's fantastically staged universe and the world's largest private collection of his works. It's an experience you'll never forget! *July/Aug daily 9am–7.15pm; Sept–June Tue–Sun 10.30am–5.10pm | admission 17 euros | A7 north (approx. 140km from Barcelona) | salvador-dali.org |* ▥ *e7*

⑤⑨ ABADIA DE MONTSERRAT 🐂

Approx. 60 mins by train (FGC: R5) from Plaça Espanya to Monistrol de Montserrat, then approx. 20 mins on the funicular

The popular Benedictine monastery of Montserrat shelters the Moreneta (black Madonna), the patron saint of Catalonia. Founded around 880, it stands on a jagged rock formation

EATING & DRINKING

Tasty treats and conviviality: the Catalans are big on food and love to combine their culinary delights: chicken with lobster, beef stew with chocolate, black paella! In this region, contrast is the name of the game with fish and seafood thrown in the pan with meat to make *mar i muntanya* – "sea and mountains".

Today, a new generation of young and experimental chefs is reinterpreting the Catalan tradition, inspired by the world-famous exponent of molecular gastronomy, Ferran Adrià. And it's been a huge success! A veritable meteor shower of Michelin stars has fallen

You'll find all the venues in this chapter on the pull-out map 🗺

Quimet & Quimet: Fine wines and delicious tapas will quickly overcome any reservations

on the region since he opened up shop. But food here doesn't have to be expensive. Countless family-run eateries and bars offer a daily good-value lunch menu, the *menú del día*: starter, main and dessert from 12 euros, often including a drink.

If you're a late eater, you've come to the right place: in the evening Catalans eat from about 9pm, at lunchtime, not before 2pm. But if you get peckish in between then luckily you can always stop for some tapas – an art at which Barcelona is proud to excel! And wash it down with a glass of *cava*, the excellent Catalan sparkling wine.

WHERE BARCELONA EATS

ABaC ★

Travessera de Dalt

Gràcia

Sant Gervasi

Via Augusta

Hofmann ★

Avinguda del Tibidabo

Avinguda Diagonal

Carrer de Pau Claris

Avinguda Diagonal

Provença Ⓜ

Compartir Barcelona ★

Eixample

Avinguda Diagonal

Carrer d'Aribau

Les Corts

CARRER D'ENRIC GRANADOS

From Argentinian steak to lemon sorbet: Barcelona's favourite restaurant area

Corts Catalanes

Ronda de Sant Pau

Carrer de Tarragona

Gran Via de les

Carrer de la Creu Coberta

Espanya Ⓜ

Poble Sec
Avinguda

Ⓜ

Quimet & Quimet ★

Sants - Montjuïc

Avinguda Diagonal

Corts Catalanes

Carrer de Pallars

Sant Martí

Tetuan

Gran Vía de les

PASSEIG DE SANT JOAN

Brunch in style: the wide pavements have cemented the promenade's position as firm favourite

AROUND THE MERCAT DE LA BARCELONETA

Tapas and fish: head to the market for the best bars

Via Laietana

Mercat de Sant Josep (La Boqueria) ★ Barceloneta

La Barceloneta

Ciutat Vella

CARRER PARLAMENT

Bar to bar: where vermouth is back in fashion

del

400 m
437 yd

BARS, CAFÉS, TAVERNS & TAPAS PLACES

1 BAR LA PLATA 🐟

This small, rustic bar with ceramic tiles and formica tables is frequented by both local residents and tourists looking for authentic ambience. Four tapas are on offer, and fried sardines are the house specialty. You won't break the bank here: glasses of wine start at 1.80 euro. *Closed Sun and Aug | C/ de la Mercé 28 | metro L4: Jaume I | Barri Gòtic | ᕲ c4*

2 BAR LEO 🚩

A quirky tapas bar that is always packed to the rafters. The songs on the jukebox aren't exactly the latest releases, but that only adds to the charm. You can order mussels, croquettes and more to go with your beer or wine. *Daily | C/ de Sant Carles 34 | tel. 932 242 071 | metro L4: Barceloneta | Barceloneta | ᕲ K12*

3 CAFÉ MAURI

Behind pretty, Art Nouveau shop windows, Barcelona's upper crust bite gleefully into all-butter croissants and bite-sized salmon snacks. The café's tartlets and chocolate delicacies are famous city-wide – and make a good souvenir! The café is quite an institution having been around since 1929. *Rambla de Catalunya 102 | tel. 932 150 998 | pasteleriasmauri.com | metro L3, L5: Diagonal | Eixample | ᕲ J7*

4 CAN DENDÊ

With its charming mix of flea-market crockery and tasty home-made food, this small breakfast café is a regular haunt for Barcelona's trendsetters. The proprietors offer friendly and relaxed service even during peak times, serving up home-made lemonade and perfectly poached eggs. You must try the pancakes with home-made fruit compote, crème fraîche and bananas – absolutely delicious. Don't forget to pet the resident dog – after all, the place is named after him. *Closed Tue/Wed | C/ de la Ciutat de Granada 44 | tel. 646 325 551 | candende.com | metro L4: Llacuna | Poplenou | ᕲ M10*

INSIDER TIP
Breakfast for a sweet tooth

5 ATLANTA

This might be the unofficial haunt of the local football club, but it also serves incredible home-made tapas based on recipes from the friendly landlady's mother, grandmother and great-grandmother. Cash only! *Closed Aug, otherwise daily | Rambla del Raval 13 | tel. 933 297 541 | metro L3: Liceu | Raval | ᕲ a2*

6 CERVECERÍA CATALANA 🚩

Popular bar classic: mountains of appetising tapas fresh from the market – around the clock. If you want to avoid the long midday queues, come for a between-meal snack. *Daily | C/ de Mallorca 236 | metro L3, L5: Diagonal | Eixample | ᕲ H8*

7 ELS QUATRE GATS

Legendary artists' haunt with an Art Nouveau ambience, where Picasso and the Catalan bohème were regulars. Traditional Catalan cooking.

Els Quatre Gats: a legendary artists' haunt frequented by Picasso

Closed Aug | C/ de Montsió 3 | tel. 933 024 140 | metro L1, L3: Catalunya | Barri Gòtic | ▭ c2

8 EL VASO DE ORO

The bar is endless, the selection of beers is vast, and the traditional tapas are delicious. For over 50 years, this bar has been an institution in the La Barceloneta area. Tired of gambas, sausages and *patates braves*? Order the *bocadillo granjero*, a sandwich lavishly topped with egg, cheese, ham, tomato and lettuce. *Closed Sept | C/ de Balboa 6 | vasodeoro.com | tel. 933 193 098 | metro L4: Barceloneta | Barceloneta | ▭ d4*

9 EL XAMPANYET 🚩

This rustic champagne bar serves cavas, wines and tasty tapas. It's an institution. *Closed Sun evening and Mon, as well as in Aug | C/ Montcada 22 | tel. 933 197 003 | metro L4: Jaume I | El Born | ▭ d3*

10 GRANJA LA PALLARESA

Xurros amb xocolata, deep-fried sticks of dough served with thick hot chocolate, are as much a part of the culinary signature of the Mediterranean metropolis as *pa amb tomàquet* and the like. Generations of Barcelonians have enjoyed the sweet treat at this Old Town staple alongside numerous sumptuous dairy desserts. Experts order a *suizo*, literally a "Swiss": a giant mountain of cool, full-fat cream is added to the sweet, pudding-like chocolate. The pinnacle of indulgence! *Mon–Sat 9am–1pm, 4–9pm, Sun 9am–1pm, 5–9pm | C/ de Petritxol 11 | tel. 933 022 036 | Metro L3: Liceu | Barri Gòtic | ▭ b2*

INSIDER TIP
Alpine dessert

11 PUDDING BARCELONA CAFÉ 🎭

Muggles are more than welcome at the this café. But be warned! Magical forces may keep you longer than

If the situation calls for bubbles, in Barcelona it can only be cava

originally planned… The selection of cheesecakes, crêpes and doorstop sandwiches are just too tempting! And the café's three floors complete with overflowing bookshelves and magical trees truly transport you to the wizarding world. On a rainy day you can while away the time in comfort playing chess and other board games. *Daily* | *Av. Diagonal 515* | *tel. 937 689 884* | *metro L3: Maria Cristina* | *Les Corts* | 🗺 *G6*

🄬 NOMAD COFFEE LAB SHOP
High-quality coffee, roasted in Barcelona and fashionably served on the counter of a bar tucked away in an arcade. Connoisseurs take theirs without sugar, and you can also order to your own taste. It's so good they opened another branch in Raval *(C/ de Joaquín Costa 26)*. *Mon–Fri 8.30am–5.30pm, closed Sat/Sun* | *Passatge Sert 12* | *tel. 628 566 235* | *nomad coffee.es* | *metro L1, L4: Urquinaona* | *Sant Pere* | 🗺 *d2*

🄭 QUIMET & QUIMET ⭐
This small, rustic bar has been famous for generations for its delicious Catalan tapas, the selected wines and the cosy familiar atmosphere. *Closed Sat evening, Sun and in Aug* | *C/ del Poeta Cabanyes 25* | *tel. 934 423 142* | *metro L2, L3: Parallel* | *Poble Sec* | 🗺 *G10*

🄮 ROCAMBOLESC
Put an imaginative three-star chef like Jordi Roca i Fontané behind the ice cream counter, and it's no surprise when he creates an edible strawberry-rosewater sorbet nose or conjures up a sweet cream with "unicorn milk". And how about cotton candy or guayaba pearls as toppings? To properly explore Jordi's world of wonder, order a *panet*, a hot filled brioche – we recommend trying it with blueberry lemon ice cream and caramel brittle. A combination to die for! *Mon noon–12.30am, Tue–Sun 11am–12.30am* | *La Rambla 51–59* | *rocambolesc.com* | *Metro L3: Liceu* | *Raval* | 🗺 *b3*

INSIDER TIP
Ice cream but better

🄯 VINITUS
Impressive option in iconic Eixample. Navajas clams, gambas and other delicacies from the sea are appetisingly

Today's specials

Starters

ESCALIVADA
Grilled vegetables (aubergine, peppers, onions) in olive oil

ESQUEIXADA
Salad with salt cod, tomatoes, onions, peppers and olives

ESPINACS A LA CATALANA
Spinach with raisins and pine nuts

AMANIDA CATALANA
Salad with cured meats and smoked sausage

Mains

SUQUET DE PEIX
Catalan fish soup with seafood and potatoes

BACALLÀ A LA SAMFAINA
Salt cod with vegetable ragout

ARRÒS NEGRE
Rice with squid including the ink, which lends the dish its black colour

FIDEUÀ
Pasta paella with fish and seafood, baked in the oven

FRICANDÓ
Veal filets simmered in mushroom sauce

MANDONGUILLES AMB SIPIA
Meatballs with squid in sauce

CANELONES A LA CATALANA
Catalan-style cannelloni, filled with mincemeat or chicken, topped with bechamel sauce and baked in the oven

Sides

PA AMB TOMÀQUET
Bread rubbed with garlic and tomato and drizzled with olive oil

ALLIOLI
Mayonnaise made with garlic and olive oil

Desserts

CREMA CATALANA
Sweet egg custard, covered with a layer of caramelised sugar

MEL I MATÓ
Cream cheese with honey

Drinks

CAVA
Catalan sparkling wine

displayed behind glass. The waiters are well-equipped to offer good advice and remain friendly, even when busy. If you're in a hurry, you can order a couple of *montaditos* – white bread topped with, for example, anchovies and roasted peppers or liver with apple confit. *C/ del Consell de Cent 333 | tel. 933 632 127 | metro L2/L3/ L4: Passeig de Gràcia | Eixample | ⊞ H8*

RESTAURANTS €€€

16 ABAC ⭐

Jordi Cruz has definitely earned his two Michelin stars. His innovative creations such as squid cannelloni or tonic bubbles accompanied by mango sorbet are artfully staged in his puristic, elegant restaurant. The way to the table leads right through the kitchen. With garden and conservatory. *Daily | Av. Tibidabo 1 | tel. 933 196 600 | abacbarcelona.com | suburban train FGC: Av. Tibidabo | Sarrià-Sant Gervasi | ⊞ H3*

17 ALKIMIA

Finest new Catalan cuisine, Michelin-starred: virtuoso chef Jordi Vila plays with taste and texture, turning traditional tomato bread into a shot of white tomato juice, topped with olive oil and toasted breadcrumbs. Elegantly styled interior. Also lunch menus. *Closed Sat lunchtime and Sun as well as in Aug and during the Easter holidays | Ronda Sant Antoni 41 | tel. 932 076 115 | alkimia.cat | metro L2: Sant Antoni | Sant Antoni | ⊞ a1*

18 COMPARTIR BARCELONA ⭐

A mix of traditional dishes such as chard salad and experiments like Thai-spiced turbot have made starred chefs Oriol Castro, Eduard Xatruch and Mateu Casañas household names in Cadaqués. This tapas restaurant brings a touch of the Costa Brava to Barcelona – not just with its menu, but also with its blue windows and lamps made of timber aged by the wind and sun. Whatever you choose, make sure you try the brioche filled with truffle and mozzarella! *Closed Mon/Tue | C/ de València 225 | tel. 936 247 886 | compartirbarcelona. com | metro L6, L7: Provença | Eixample | ⊞ H8*

19 DISFRUTAR

Gourmet-lovers and fans of experimental cooking will appreciate the avant-garde cuisine created by the three young master chefs – Mateu Casañas, Oriol Castro and Eduard Xatruch. They trained with star chef Ferran Adrià at the world-famous El Bulli. This establishment is among the ten best restaurants in the world. Reserve ahead online. *Tue–Sat 1–3pm and 8–10pm | C/ de Villarroel 163 | tel. 933 486 896 | disfrutarbarcelona. com | metro L5: Hospital Clinic | Eixample | ⊞ G7*

20 DOS PEBROTS

Sorry? A tortilla with pine nuts, honey and that fish sauce from *The Adventures of Asterix*? Yes, that's right! Garum, the fermented seasoning invented

INSIDER TIP Garum is the secret!

by the Romans, tastes just great here and is served up with amusing historical facts. Chef Albert Raurich draws inspiration from old paintings and historic cookbooks, and even seeks advice from archaeologists. He also provides amateur historians with information about origins and preparation methods on the menu. If you want to learn more then ask the staff! *Wed/Thu 7.30–11.30pm, Fri–Sun 1.30–4pm and 7.30–11.30pm | C/ del Doctor Dou 19 | tel. 938 539 598 | dospebrots.com | metro L3: Liceu | Raval | ⬚ b2*

21 GAIG

Top chef Carles Gaig combines traditional Catalan cooking with up-to-date haute cuisine. Pleasantly laid-back restaurant with an excellent wine list, a Michelin star – and still affordable menus from 75 euros. *Tue–Sun 10am–4pm | C/ de la Nau Santa Maria 5 | tel. 934 291 017 | restaurantgaig. com | metro L3: Maria Cristina | Sarrià | ⬚ F5*

22 GRESCA

Young chef Rafael Peña, one of the gastronomic discoveries of recent years, is enriching Catalan cuisine with surprising ideas such as octopus carpaccio with black pudding or duck with prawns (photo). The small restaurant has simple furnishings and a friendly attitude. ☛ Recommended lunch menu for 21 euros. *Closed Sat lunchtime and Sun | C/ de Provença 230 | tel. 934 516 193 | gresca.net | metro L3, L5: Diagonal | Eixample | ⬚ H7*

23 HOFMANN ★

Many famous chefs de cuisine have emerged from May Hofmann's school

Smoked duck roll with marinated prawns and mustard leaves, anyone?

of high cuisine. The Michelin-starred food tastes of imagination and sophistication. Lunch menu. *Closed Sat, Sun, public holidays and in Aug | C/ de la Granada del Penedés 14–16 | tel. 932 187 165 | hofmann-bcn.com | metro L3, L5: Diagonal | Sarrià-Sant Gervasi | ▥ H6*

24 MANAIRÓ

Manairons are a Catalonian variety of gnome or pixie, and it's entirely possible that they are hard at work behind the scenes here, since the hustle and bustle in the kitchen is completely concealed from the guests at this intimately lit, high-quality restaurant. Exquisite Catalonian cuisine from Jordi Herrera. *Closed Sun | C/ de la Diputació 424 | tel. 932 310 057 | manairo.com | metro L2: Monumental | Eixample | ▥ L8*

25 MOMENTS

For her gentle modernisation of Catalan cuisine, Carme Ruscalleda was crowned – as the only female cook worldwide – with seven Michelin stars. She seems to have passed on her talent to her son Raül Balam. Together, in the Hotel Mandarin, they take their guests on a gourmet trip from Barcelona via Tokyo to Marrakech. *Closed Sun, Mon | Passeig de Gràcia 38–40 | tel. 931 518 781 | mandarin oriental.es | metro L2, L3, L4: Passeig de Gràcia | Eixample | ▥ J8*

26 PALO VERDE

That waft of charcoal appeals to all our deepest instincts, but when Uruguayan chef Andrés Bluth adds Japanese-inspired meat skewers or pig ears to it, the smell will appeal to even the most distinguished of gourmets. *Closed Sun/Mon | Còrsega 232 | tel. 932 376 998 | hotelomm.es | metro L6, L7: Provença | Eixample | ▥ H7*

27 COME BY PACO MÉNDEZ

"Eat!": the prompt in the restaurant's name couldn't really be clearer. And Paco Méndez certainly offers enough options to choose from. Over the last five years, the star chef has developed 500 recipes – all new interpretations of classic Mexican recipes like ceviche with gambas or tacos reimagined for the gourmet palette! The only downside is the price: the tasting menu costs 130 euros. Booking compulsory. *Closed Sun/Mon | Av. de Mistral 54 | tel. 938 275 977 | come. com.es | metro L1, L3: Espanya | San Antoni | ▥ F9*

28 ENIGMA

The pandemic hit the Adrià family's culinary empire hard. Now, they have reopened their flagship restaurant in an attempt to rise from the ashes: the ambience is more relaxed and the prices lower than you might expect in starred restaurants. Instead of a tasting menu, there are mini menus with recipes from El Bulli's molecular kitchen as well as classics prepared with more than a dash of high-tech and innovative spirit. *Mon–Fri 6.30–10.30pm | C/ Sepúlveda 38 | tel. 616 696 322 | enigmaconcept. es | metro L1: Rocafort | Sant Antoni | ▥ F9*

29 TUNATECA BALFEGÓ

Glittering silver mobiles, rippling blue curtains and ceramic mosaics more than a little reminiscent of scales – you guessed it! It's all about the fish here! Specifically, the red tuna. Whether it's sashimi, carpaccio or steak, whatever the Balfegó family serves will leave your taste buds craving "more sea". The tuna is sourced from the family's own sustainable fishing business – and the interior design is from a local award-winning studio. *Closed Sun | Av. Diagonal 439, in the lobby of Hotel Omm | tel. 937 976 460 | tunateca balfego.com | metro L3, L5: Diagonal | Eixample | ⸿ H6*

30 XIRINGUITO ESCRIBÀ

This restaurant right on Bogatell beach is famous for its rice and pasta stir-fries. The daily menu includes fish and seafood straight off the boat. *Oct–May closed in the evenings | Av. Litoral Mar 42 | tel. 932 210 729 | escriba.es | metro L4: Llacuna | Poblenou | ⸿ M11*

RESTAURANTS €€

31 1881 PER SAGARDI

The view alone deserves three stars! From the rooftop terrace of the Museum of Catalan History, the panorama sweeps over the Old Port, taking in the rooftops of the Old Town. But this is not a restaurant that will let you forget the food! Don't miss the painstakingly prepared fish and meat options or the delicious rice dishes. If you're not in the mood for a slap-up dinner, come in between mealtimes and order some *patatas bravas*. The fried potato chunks with their spicy sauce are among the best in town. *Pl. de Pau Vila 3 | tel. 679 202 040 | gruposagardi. com | metro L4: Barceloneta | Barceloneta | ⸿ c4*

INSIDER TIP
Bravo for the bravas

32 BAR LOBO

Don't let the name fool you: the "bar" is actually a restaurant, and one with a

So the guests are all seated and nobody's at the bar? No wonder, Bar Lobo is really a restaurant

nice terrace in the trendy Raval district to boot. The delicious dishes are sometimes Mediterranean-, sometimes Japanese-inspired. Watch the sushi chefs hard at work on the upper floor, or soak in the urban ambience with a seat downstairs. *Daily | C/ del Pintor Fortuny 3 | tel. 934 815 346 | grupotragaluz.com | metro L1, L2: Pl. Catalunya | Raval | ▥ b2*

▨ BESTIAL

Its large and pretty terrace with sea views makes this beach bistro a hot tip for summer nights. Italian cuisine. *Daily | C/ de Ramón Trias Fargas 2–4 | tel. 932 240 407 | grupotragaluz.com | metro L4: Ciutadella | Barceloneta | ▥ L11*

▨ CUINES DE SANTA CATERINA

At the stalls of this innovatively renovated market hall Santa Caterina you can have breakfast or gorge yourself on Mediterranean, Asian or vegetarian tapas. Everything here is fresh from the market. *Daily | Mercat de Santa Caterina | Av. Francesc Cambó 16 | tel. 932 689 918 | cuinessanta caterina.com | metro L4: Jaume I | Ribera | ▥ c3*

▨ ELS TRES PORQUETS

If you're exploring off-the-beaten (read tourist) path, you'd be lucky to stumble into a place like this: families and friends chatter happily away at the wooden tables over feasts of meatballs with squid, cabbage rolls and other market-fresh Catalan classics. To guests unfamiliar with the area, the host will happily sign and gesticulate with what looks like his entire body to explain the menu on the blackboard, which is written only in *catañol*, an adventurous mix of Spanish and Catalan. After the feast, you won't just leave full and happy, but also richer by two or three Spanish-Catalan expressions. *Closed Sun | Rambla del Poblenou 165 | tel. 933 008 750 | elstresporquets.es | metro L1: Glòries | Poblenou | ▥ N9*

INSIDER TIP
Lunch with language lessons

▨ EN VILLE

Mirrors, marble tables and 1920s decor in the style of a French bistro. Good Mediterranean and market-fresh food. Always jam-packed around lunchtime, thanks to the popular and very reasonably priced 🍴 lunch menu! *Closed Sun evening and Mon evening | C/ del Doctor Dou 14 | tel. 933 028 467 | envillebarcelona.es | metro L1, L3: Catalunya | Raval | ▥ b2*

▨ FLAX & KALE

Unrendered brick walls and quinoa salad: the combination of attractive design and healthy, tasty food available here appeals to more than just vegans and vegetarians. The rooftop terrace and herb garden makes a particularly pleasant setting for dinner, and make sure you try the vegetable juices! The branch in Sant Pere *(C/ Sant Pere Més Alt 31–33)* also has delicious fish options on the menu. *Daily | C/ Tallers 74B | tel. 933 175 664 | teresacarles.com/fk | metro L1, L2: Universitat | Raval | ▥ b1*

38 9 GRANADOS

The tapas have zing, the vegetables are crunchy, and the fish menu features Catalan and Basque classics, plus a touch of Asia. The owners have long been a part of Barcelona's gourmet scene, but this restaurant is a project particularly close to their hearts. And you can taste that! If you're lucky, you'll get a seat on the terrace. *Daily | C/ d'Enric Granados 9 | tel. 934 531 120 | 9granados.com | metro L1: Universitat | Eixample | ⊞ H8*

39 LA POLPA

The menu strikes the perfect balance between tradition and cosmopolitan sophistication. In addition to Catalan classics like *canelons* (stuffed dough rolls) or *butifarra* (fried sausage), the tube-like restaurant also serves red curry and Mexican tacos. Everything is cooked to perfection. *Closed Mon evening | C/ d'Enric Granados 69 | tel. 933 238 308 | metro L3, L5: Diagonal | Eixample | ⊞ H7*

40 LA VENTA

Even in winter you can enjoy the views from Tibidabo on the heated terraces of this pretty Art Nouveau restaurant, while tucking into Mediterranean dishes. Booking recommended! *Closed Sun evening | Plaça Doctor Andreu | tel. 932 126 455 | restaurante laventa.com | metro Tibidabo, last stop of Tramvía Blau or bus no. 196 (until 10pm) | Sarrià-Sant Gervasi | ⊞ J2*

41 LLAMBER

A successful Asturian–Catalan joint venture. She's to thank for the high, light, brick walls and interior design; he reigns supreme in the kitchen. Whether it's beetroot carpaccio with pistachio, or cod with honey and mead sausage, the dishes taste first-class and cleverly combine culinary traditions. The Spanish Northeast and Northwest come together once again in beautiful harmony on the cheese board. We recommend the breakfast menu! *Daily | C/ de la Fusina 5 | tel. 933 196 250 | llamber.com | metro L3: Liceu, L4: Jaume | El Born | ⊞ d3*

42 MERCAT DE SANT JOSEP (LA BOQUERIA) ★ ⚑

Locals also enjoy eating at the Boqueria market. The *Pinotxo* counter *(closed Sun | stall 466–470)* of city-wide fame

Healthy and tasty: the Raval's Flax & Kale serves amazing plant-based food

attracts even top chefs after their market shop. A culinary institution with a price tag to match. Try the daily menu at the counter of *Kiosko Universal (closed Sun | stall 691)*, always crowded at lunchtime, or *El Quim de la Boqueria (closed Sun and Mon | stall 584)* for authentic gourmet fare. *Metro L3: Liceu | Raval | ⌘ b2*

43 MINYAM

Don't worry! If it suddenly starts smoking and steaming, the chef hasn't fallen asleep. More likely is that the next table has ordered the house special: *arroz Vulcanus*, rosemary-smoked paella, and exactly the kind of experimental success that has made fashionable Poblenou so popular with trendsetters. Just so you know, the restaurant's name isn't a reference to some southeast Asian city, but the name of a lima ginger sauce created by the resourceful owner, which is still awaiting the patent. *Closed Mon | C/ de Pujades 187 | tel. 933 483 618 | metro L4: Poblenou | Poblenou | ⌘ N10*

44 ARUME

Author Manuel Vázquez Montalbán was not just famous for his Pepe Carvalho crime novels, but also for his love of great food. In a lovely tribute to the writer, who died in 2003, one of the city's best Galician restaurants now resides in the house where he was born. The squid on potato foam, finely flavoured with lime, is simply divine! *Wed–Sun 7–11pm, Fri–Sun also*

INSIDER TIP
Criminally good!

1–3pm | C/ Botella 11 | tel. 933 154 872 | arumerestaurant.com | metro L2: San Antoni | Raval | ⌘ a2

45 RASOTERRA

Creative and undogmatic vegetarian dishes made with organic, home-grown produce. The owners of this pleasant restaurant subscribe to the slow-food movement. Tapas, daily specials, brunch on Saturday and Sunday. *Closed Mon | C/ de Palau 5 | tel. 933 186 926 | rasoterra.cat | metro L4: Jaume I | Barri Gòtic | ⌘ c3*

46 L'AMFORA

In Barcelona, it's usually best to write off any restaurants aggressively advertised with the buzzword *"paella"* as catering to the tourist masses. Not so in this family-run establishment: the rice dishes are delicious, the prices fair, and the waiters attentive and friendly.

Pinotxo in La Boqueria market hall: a simple counter, but haute cuisine

But do book! *Daily | Av. del Paral·lel 184 | tel. 626 846 369 | metro L1: Pl. Espanya | Sant Antoni | ▢ F9*

47 SET PORTES

A gastronomic institution, famous for its paellas, serving traditional Catalan food in cosy Old Town atmosphere, only a few steps from the port. *Daily | Passeig Isabel II 14 | tel. 933 193 033 | 7portes.com | metro L4: Barceloneta | Ribera | ▢ c4*

48 SILENUS

Charming restaurant in the vicinity of the Museum of Contemporary Art. Lovingly prepared culinary culture from all around the Mediterranean with a relaxed ambience. Plus, changing art exhibitions will cater to the eye, too. *Closed Sun | C/ dels Àngels 8 | tel. 933 022 680 | restaurantsilenus.com | metro L1, L3: Catalunya | Raval | ▢ b2*

RESTAURANTS €

49 EL MANABA

Starving but skint? A dilemma this Ecuadorian restaurant knows well. The solution? The weekday, low-priced lunch menus for 10 euros or the *platos combinados*, mixed plates with rice, yucca, salad, fish or meat. All tasty and freshly prepared. The carbohydrate-rich meals could easily see you up the ascent of Mount Cotopaxi – or, more conveniently, Tibidabo! *Daily | C/ de Provença 351 | tel. 931 438 897 | elmanaba.es | metro L4: Verdaguer | Sagrada Família | ▢ K7*

50 CAN MAÑO

This restaurant in Barceloneta looks like the set for an Italian film from the 1960s. The fresh fish is prepared simply and lovingly. Book a table in good time, if you want to beat the tour groups and locals. *Mon and Sat 8.30am–4pm, Tue–Fri 8.30am–4pm and 8–11pm, closed Sun | C/ Baluard 12 | tel. 933 193 082 | metro L4: Barceloneta | Barceloneta | ⊞ K11*

51 JOANET

Let the neighbours cook ceviche, pizza and other new-fangled cosmopolitan hits. The landlady of this friendly bar in El Born has been cooking what she does best for decades: sardines, mussels, croquettes and Catalan classics such as *mongetes amb botifarra*, sausage with beans. No wonder the clientele is staunchly loyal and on a first-name terms with the owner. Cosy summer evenings are guaranteed under the plane trees around the lantern fountain. *Tue–Sun 9am–4pm, Fri/Sat also 8–11.30pm | Plaça de Sant Agustí Vell 6 | tel. 933 199 037 | joanet.es | metro L1: Arc de Triomf | El Born | ⊞ d2*

INSIDER TIP
Romantic spot

52 GAT BLAU

The young team belongs to the Slow Food movement and places great value on organic ingredients, fair trade and regional products. The meals are simple, but varied and delicious; the atmosphere is friendly and relaxed. *Tue 1–4pm, Wed–Sat 1–4pm and 8.30–10.30pm | Consell del Cent 139 | tel. 933 256 199 | gat blau.com | metro L1: Rocafort | Eixample | ⊞ G8*

53 GELIDA 🐖

A veritable establishment serving traditional Catalan home cooking at unbeatable value for money: almost all dishes cost less than 4 euros! The family-run restaurant is nearly always packed, and they don't take bookings. But if you speak a little Spanish or Catalan, you have a good chance of charming the resolute landlady and securing a seat. *Closed Sat evenings and Sun | Comte d'Urgell 75 | tel. 9 34 53 10 61 | metro L1: Urgell | Eixample | ⊞ G8*

54 LA BELLA NAPOLI

Excellent stone-baked pizzas, as authentically Italian as the ambience, service and atmosphere. This is a popular restaurant, including with families with children, so book or go early in the evening. *Daily | C/ de Margarit 14 | tel. 934 425 056 | bella napoli.es | metro L3: Poble Sec | Poble Sec | ⊞ G10*

55 LA BOMBETA

Here at this rustic eatery in the fishing village of Barceloneta the *bombetas*, little bombs, that gave the place its name, are still home-made: fried balls of mashed potato with a meat filling, hot sauce and aioli. The grilled hake or calamari are also very tasty. No credit cards. *Closed Wed | C/ de la Maquinista 3 | tel. 933 199 445 | metro L4: Barceloneta | Barceloneta | ⊞ J11*

56 LA COVA FUMADA

A true classic in the Barceloneta quarter. This restaurant on the square in front of the market hall serves the house wine in vast glass jugs, while the landlady cooks up *bombetas* and *croquetas* made to her family recipe.

Tried and tested: Can Culleretes has been serving Catalan food for over 230 years

The simple marble tables are as much a part of the authentic ambience as the ancient blackboard that lists the catch of the day and price. *Mon–Fri 9am–3.15pm and Thu/Fri 6–8.15pm, Sat 9am–1pm, closed Sun | C/ del Baluart 56 | tel. 932 214 061 | metro L4: Barceloneta | Barceloneta | ⌖ J11*

57 LA FONDA

This modern version of the traditional Catalonian guesthouse is very popular with non-guests for its lunch menu. Reservations can only be made online. *Daily | Escudellers 10 | andilana.com/ en/locales/la-fonda-3 | metro L3: Drassanes | Barri Gòtic | ⌖ b3*

58 LA DOLÇA HERMINIA

From pasta to curry, the menu provides everything you need to leave satisfied and full. The ambience is lively, the portions large and the prices more than reasonable. *Daily | C/ de les Magdalenes 27 | tel. 933 170 676 | metro L1, L3: Pl. Catalunya | Casc Antic | ⌖ c2*

59 CAN CULLERETES

Opened in 1786, this guesthouse is not only the oldest in town, but it does offer sound Catalan cuisine at a good price. Never tried the tender beef stew *fricandó*? Then definitely order it here! *Closed Mon | C/ Quintana 5 | tel. 933 173 022 | metro L3: Liceu | culleretes.com | Ciutat Vella | ⌖ b3*

SHOPPING

Whether you're after hip design, vintage clothes or casual urban fashion, then you're in the right place. El Born, Raval and Gràcia are havens for fashion victims and design lovers who can browse delightful boutiques to their heart's content – and the "Made in Barcelona" sign is almost a matter of course in the shop windows here. If you're more into Armani and Louis Vuitton, then you can find luxury brands in the area around Passeig de Gràcia.

There's not much point picking up flamenco castanets or sombreros here – first, because they're about as typical of Barcelona as a full

You'll find all the venues in this chapter on the pull-out map 📖

Former bullring turned shopping centre: the Arenas de Barcelona

English, and second, because you'll find much nicer souvenirs in museum shops and design stores. Watch out: the trainers, jerseys and handbags laid out on the rugs of dealers looking to make a quick quid at the port and in the metro stations are guaranteed to be fake, and buying them can be punishable with a fine.

Usual shop opening hours are Monday to Saturday between 10am and 2.30pm and again from 4.30 to 8pm. The major shopping centres and department stores are usually open until 10pm, many without a siesta.

WHERE TO SHOP IN BARCELONA

MARCO POLO HIGHLIGHTS

★ **OLD TOWN**
Browse Barcelona's most interesting antique shops ➤ p. 86

★ **CASA GISPERT**
A general store that'll transport you back to your great-grandmother's time ➤ p. 87

★ **ART ESCUDELLERS**
Stylish Catalan arts and crafts: from tiles and ceramics to original jewellery ➤ p. 88

★ **OMG BCN**
Unique and beautiful hand-crafted gifts ➤ p. 90

★ **TEXTILE ROUTE**
Modern designs within medieval walls ➤ p. 90

★ **MERCAT DE SANT JOSEP**
Sensual shopping experience – the "belly of Barcelona" ➤ p. 90

★ **LA MANUAL ALPARGATERA**
Traditional, custom-made espadrilles ➤ p. 93

CARRER DELS TALLERS
Flea-market fashion and vinyl rarities

ARENAS DE BARCELONA
Shopping centre in a former bullring, with an amazing view of Montjuïc

DOMINICAL DE LLIBRES
The Sunday book market in the Mercat de Sant Antoni is bursting with tradition

Diagonal Ⓜ

Carrer de Pau Claris

Carrer de Balmes

Carrer d'Aragó

Carrer d'Aragó

Universitat Ⓜ

Gran Via de les Corts Catalanes

Ronda de

Sant Antoni Ⓜ

Sant Pau

Espanya Ⓜ

Avinguda del Paral·lel

Avinguda del Paral·lel

Sants-Montjuïc

Eixample

PASSEIG DE GRÀCIA

Gucci, Cartier, Dolce & Gabbana: the crème de la crème of designers woo their clientele on Barcelona's most expensive street

Gran Via de les Corts Catalanes

Ⓜ Passeig de Gràcia

OLD TOWN

Pedestrianised zones Portal de l'Àngel and Portaferissa are home to the big chains

Urquinaona Ⓜ

TEXTILE ROUTE

Original fashion, made in Barcelona, surrounds the Carrer Banys Vells

Catalunya Ⓜ

OMG BCN ★ 📍
Textile Route ★ 📍
Jaume I Ⓜ
Casa Gispert ★ 📍

Old Town ★ 📍

Via Laietana

Mercat de Sant Josep (La Boqueria) ★ 📍   Ⓜ Liceu

La Manual Alpargatera ★ 📍

Ciutat Vella   Art Escudellers ★ 📍

Ronda Litoral

LITTLE SOHO IN THE RAVAL

Pop-up shops, up-and-coming designers and bric-à-brac for hipsters

200 m
219 yd

ANTIQUES

Barcelona is a mecca for (well-off) lovers of Catalan Art Nouveau. The less well-heeled visitors will enjoy browsing around the *Els Encants* flea market.

1 OLD TOWN ★

You can wander around the atmospheric antique shops in the medieval alleys of the former Jewish quarter of El Call. The most interesting shops here are in the Carrer de la Palla and in the Carrer dels Banys Nous. *Barri Gòtic | ⅏ c3*

BOOKS

If you're looking for art or coffee-table books, the museum bookshops offer an excellent selection, especially those of the Miró Foundation, the Picasso Museum or the Centre for Contemporary Culture.

WHERE TO START?

Although the **Plaça de Catalunya** *(⅏ c1-2)* with El Corte Inglés on the west side and the bulky shopping centre on the east side won't win any beauty contests, the central square is an ideal starting point, because the main shopping streets lead off from here: the **Portal de l'Àngel** *(⅏ c2)*, the **Passeig de Gràcia** *(⅏ c1–2)* and the **Rambla de Catalunya** *(⅏ b1-4)*. Tip: Go in search of independent boutiques in the side streets. Barcelona is full of them!

2 ABRACADABRA 😜

If you need to stock up on books for the kids, this bookshop specialises in children's and young adult literature. They also sell foreign-language books and a selection of beautiful toys. *General Álvarez de Castro 5 | metro L4: Jaume I | La Ribera | ⅏ c2*

3 LA CENTRAL DEL RAVAL

This Baroque chapel houses one of the largest and best-stocked bookshops in Europe. It even has a small selection of foreign-language works. *C/ d'Elisabets 6 | lacentral.com | metro L1, L3: Catalunya | Raval | ⅏ b2*

DELICACIES & SPECIALITIES

4 CACAO SAMPAKA

Pure cocoa culture, without additives: chocolate in surprising creations and aromas. With a café. *Café Mon–Sat 10am–8.30pm | C/ del Consell de Cent 292 | cacaosampaka.com | metro L2, L3, L4: Passeig de Gràcia | Eixample | ⅏ J8*

5 CAELUM ☂

The beautifully arranged pastries in the shop window are sure to make any passerby's mouth water, while the range of marzipans, wines and liqueurs will cause even die-hard agnostics to waver, because everything sold here is made in Spanish monasteries and convents. Try church wines and monastery pastries by candlelight in the restored 14th-century cellar. *Daily noon–8pm | C/ de la Palla*

8 | Instagram: @caelumbcn | metro L3: Liceu | Barri Gòtic | ⌑ b3

6 CASA GISPERT ★

Enchanting general store, over 150 years old, in the Ribera quarter. The oven where prunes and apricots are dried has been functioning since 1851 and is unique in all of Spain. *Closed Sun and Mon | Sombrerers 23 | casa gispert.com | metro L4: Jaume I | Ribera | ⌑ d3*

7 COLMADO QUILEZ

How to choose between the tins of fish with their pretty, nostalgic packaging, the award-winning olive oil or the top Priorat wine? Pick all three! This former general store has been a first stop for gourmets since 1908. Modernist interiors and expert advice are included for free! *Closed Sun | Rambla Catalunya 65 | lafuente.es | metro L3: Passeig de Gràcia | Eixample | ⌑ J8*

8 LA PINEDA

Tapas, sausage, wine: Catalonian delicacies are sold over the counter in this magical old general store. If you buy the *ibérico* as a souvenir, have it shrink-wrapped ready to fly! *Mon–Sat 9am–3pm and 6–9.30pm, Sun 11am–3pm | C/ del Pi 16 | metro L3: Liceu | Barri Gòtic | ⌑ b3*

9 ORO LÍQUIDO

If you've ever tasted extra virgin olive oil, you'll know why it's called "liquid gold". In this store of the same name, the oils are nicely displayed on pretty shelves. The expert staff can explain the differences between dozens of

Casa Gispert: serving up specialities from around the world

varieties as well as the 20 protected cultivation areas in Spain. The range is rounded off by an exquisite selection of natural cosmetics, made, of course, from olives.

INSIDER TIP
Full-bodied!

If you are interested in learning to taste the difference between the Arbequina and Picual varieties of olive, you can sign up for a tasting workshop. *C/ de La Palla 8 | tel. 933 022 980 | oroliquido.com | metro L4: Jaume I | Barri Gòtic | ⌑ b3*

10 PAPA BUBBLE

This sweet shop in El Born certainly has the "oooh" factor. First, for the sheer beauty of the jewel-like sweets on the shelves; second, for the variety and intensity of flavour; and third, for the masters at work twisting and shaping the strands of sugar with true skill and panache. *C/ Ample 28 | Mon-Fri 10am-2pm and 4-8.30pm | papabubble.com | metro: L4 Jaume I | Barri Gòtic | ▥ b3*

11 PASTELERÍA ESCRIBÀ ☂

A historic Art Nouveau patisserie with a richly ornate façade, one of the best places in Barcelona for those who love chocolate and all things sweet. Plus, plenty of options to take home as presents. *Daily 9am-9pm | La Rambla 83 | escriba.es | metro L3: Liceu | Raval | ▥ b3*

12 VILA VINITECA

Alongside top wines from the Priorat or cult vintages such as Vega Sicilia, there are 6,000 other wines for sale, plus a rich selection of sherry, vermouth and other rarities. *Closed Sun | C/ Agullers 7 | metro L4: Jaume I | El Born | ▥ c4*

DESIGN & ARTS & CRAFTS

13 ART ESCUDELLERS ★

Authentic handicrafts, be it traditional or contemporary, at reasonable prices. Alongside beautiful tiles there are ceramics and glass pieces, as well as original jewellery. Too fragile to risk in your luggage? the friendly staff are more than happy to take care of the shipping. *C/ dels Escudellers 23; other stores: C/ Avinyó 23, C/ Petrixol 8, C/ Banys Nous 14, Pl. de l'Àngel 2 |*

Super cellar: the wine bottles are stacked to the ceiling at Vila Viniteca

escudellers-art.com | metro L3:
Drassanes | Barri Gòtic | ◫ b3

14 B DE BARCELONA

Sadly, you can't take the whole incred-

INSIDER TIP
Design classics

ible city home with you. This shop, how-ever, is a good option for more practical souvenirs, such as Gaudí's famous hexagonal floor tiles reproduced as coasters by the original company Escofet. It's also a good choice for other "made in Barcelona" design classics, like the elegant glass oil dis-penser by Marquina. *Av. de Gaudí 28 | bdebarcelona.cat | metro L2: Sagrada Família | Eixample | ◫ L7*

15 DOS I UNA

Creative handicrafts, curiosities and quality design from Catalunya. *C/ del Rosselló 275 | metro L3, L5: Diagonal | Eixample | ◫ J7*

16 GREY STREET

Original shops selling all kinds of chic knick-knacks are the reason why some have dubbed the streets around Carrer Pintor Fortuny, Doctor Dou and Peu de la Creu "Barcelona's SoHo". And this shop is a good pitstop for design-conscious souvenir hunters. The ceramics, prints and textiles are all made by local artists. *C/ Peu de la Creu 25 | greystreetbarcelona.com | metro L2: Sant Antoni | Raval | ◫ a2*

17 KLAP

Have you just whiled away a few hours in front of MACBA, marvelling open-mouthed at the feats of the

Calorie-counters:
sweet treats at Pastelería Escribà

international skater community? Then this concept store is the place for you. For a truly individual souvenir, print a T-shirt with your very own design at the "Shirt Bar". *Carrer del Lleó 28 | klap shop.com | metro L1/L2: Universitat | Raval | ◫ a1*

18 ORÍGENS BARCELONA

Love shopping, hate the carbon foot-print? Keep your conscience clear here! From leather water bottles to backpacks made from recycled kite sails, each and every product has been made with sustainability in mind by designers from Barcelona and the surrounding area. *C/ de Felip Neri 1 | origensbcn.com | metro L4: Jaume I | Ciutat Vella | ◫ c3*

19 OMG BCN ★

"Oh my God" (OMG) is supposedly how patrons respond to the sight of the innovative gifts or original decorative items sold at this concept store. Everything is "made in Barcelona" – designed by locals and crafted by hand. *Plaça de la Llana 7 | omgbcn. com | metro L4: Jaume I | La Ribera | ▥ c3*

20 TEXTILE ROUTE ★

Let the wooden signposts lead you into El Born! The tiny alleys are home to fashion designers, hat makers, paper and jewellery artists, and shoemakers. There are very interesting shops selling original products especially in the historic artisan houses and weaving mills in the streets of Banys Vells, Esquirol Flassaders and Barra de Ferro. Just one thing: many shops are closed on Mondays. *Metro L4: Jaume I | El Born | ▥ c3*

MARKETS

21 MERCAT DELS ENCANTS

You may not discover a lost Picasso masterpiece here, but you will find all kinds of knick-knacks, attractive 🐷 bric-à-brac at bargain prices, secondhand clothes, decorative objects, jewellery, antiques and vintage gear. Barcelona's oldest and biggest flea market extends over several floors underneath an enormous reflective roof. *Mon, Wed, Fri, Sat 9am–8pm | Av. Meridiana 69 | at the Plaça de les Glòries | encantsbcn.com | metro L1: Glòries, L2: Encants | Eixample | ▥ M9*

22 MERCAT DE SANT JOSEP (LA BOQUERIA) ★ 🌴

Piled-up fresh fish and seafood, mouth-watering mounds of mushrooms, chillies, nuts and truffles: strolling through Bareclona's famous market hall on La Rambla, you understand why it is also called La Boqueria, the "Belly of Barcelona". OK, with fruit juices, tasting bags and lunch boxes, the market increasingly caters for tourists, but a stroll through the Boqueria is still a must of any visit to Barcelona. Try the delicacies at the food stalls, but not at lunchtime when it's packed to the rafters. *Closed Sun | Rambla 91 | metro L3: Liceu | Raval | ▥ b2*

23 PALO ALTO MARKET

Organic burgers and paella sizzle away in the food trucks, while relaxed electro-pop plays in the background. You can find beard wax for him and wood-framed sunglasses for her or quirky romper suits for the little ones here. On the first weekend of every month this overgrown factory site in Poblenou is transformed into a hipster paradise. The ivy-covered brick buildings are even home to Javier Mariscal, the creative mind behind the Olympic mascot Cobi. But the designer is also a passionate amateur chef. If you're lucky, you can buy a portion of his famous paella. Just ask for him at the entrance to the canteen in the large brick building! *Sat/Sun 11am–9pm | admission 5 euros | C/ dels Pellaires 30 | paloaltomarket.com | metro L4: Selva de Mar | Poblenou | ▥ O10*

INSIDER TIP
Olympic paella

If you get peckish, the food trucks at the Palo Alto Market are a great option for tasty treats

FASHION & ACCESSORIES

24 AMAPOLA

The shop in the Gràcia quarter, committed to animal welfare and the preservation of nature, offers an original alternative to conventional leatherware. No animal had to give its life for the creatively styled shoes, handbags, belts or purses made out of recycled material. *Closed Mon mornings | Travessera de Gràcia 129 | amapolaveganshop.com | metro L3: Fontana | Gràcia | ⑩ J6*

25 CUSTO

Colourful prints and a mix of materials: the innovative skirts, dresses, tops and T-shirts by Custo Dalmau's fashion label are now available in more than 50 countries, and have been copied time and again. Find the originals here, including past collections, and at reasonable prices. *Plaça del Pi 2 | custo.com | metro L4: Jaume I | El Born | ⑩ d3*

26 DESIGUAL

Patchwork clothing with the craziest combinations of fabric and colours! You can save up to 50 per cent at the outlet. Several branches. *C/ Diputació 323 | desigual.com | metro L2, L3: Passeig de Gràcia, L4: Girona | Eixample | ⑩ K8*

27 FLAMINGOS VINTAGE KILO RAVAL 🐷

At this place, you pay by weight for cool, recycled vintage clothes that are 100% made in the USA – with prices starting at 13 euros per kilo! This cult store imports large quantities and passes on the savings to its customers. Opened after the other branches in the hipster quarter of Raval

No-go zone for purists: at Desigual, wild patterns and crazy colours are the order of the day

(C/ Ferlandina 20 | metro L1, L3: Catalunya | ⊞ a2) and *Carrer Tallers (C/ Tallers 31 | metro L1, L3: Catalunya | ⊞ H9)*, *Flamingos Club (C/ Avinyó 24 | metro L3: Drassanes | Cuitat Vella | ⊞ J10)* takes things to the next level. Here, you can take a break from browsing the rails to tuck into some sushi and a cocktail or two. *vintagekilo.com*

🄲🄸 GREENLIFESTYLE

This pleasant, environmentally friendly shop in the Gràcia quarter only carries clothing that meets ecological, Fair Trade and sustainability criteria. *Torrent de l'Olla 95 | greenlifestyle.es | metro L3: Fontana | Gràcia | ⊞ J6*

🄲🄽 SANTA EULÀLIA

It was the cloth trade that made Barcelona rich and famous – and this luxury store on Passeig de Gràcia keeps the tradition alive. The city's bourgeoisie has had suits tailored here for generations – head to the basement to watch a tailor at work. Decorating the rails are fine designer pieces for him and her – from Alexander McQueen to Valentino. *Passeig de Gràcia 93 | santaeulalia. com | metro L3, L5: Diagonal | Eixample | ⊞ J7*

🄲🄾 OLOKUTI

Regional craftmanship, certified Fair Trade goods and many ecologically friendly products can be found among the clothing, accessories, jewellery and cosmetics sold here. The numerous rooms in this beautiful old house are a great place to browse, but make sure you go in the back way. The Fair Trade ginger tea tastes twice as good at the pretty mosaic tables in the lush green patio. Pleasure for the palate, soul and conscience!

INSIDER TIP
Fair Trade oasis

C/ d'Astúries 36–38 | olokuti.com | metro L3: Fontana | *Gràcia* | ⎕ J6

31 LISA LEMPP

The woman you'll see cutting and sewing leather behind the windows of this Old Town eatery is Lisa Lempp. The Swiss-born designer has been creating and sewing handbags since 1999 and now has a fiercely loyal clientele from New York to Tokyo. No wonder, really: her top-notch products are a touch of that casual-urban Mediterranean ambience that has put Barcelona on the map. *Carrer dels Mercaders 11 | lisalempp.com | metro L4: Jaume I | Casc Antic | ⎕ c3*

32 SUNO

Unusual handmade creations from local designers in the trendy quarter of El Born – from jackets and dresses to necklaces made of colourful electric cables. *Closed Mon | Cotoners 12 | metro L4: Jaume I | El Born | ⎕ c3*

SHOES

33 CAMPER

These trendy and eminently wearable shoes from the Balearics are now famous all over the world, and for good reason. Not only are they chic, but they will also last you a lifetime. Spain, the country of manufacture, offers a particularly large selection. Camper now also produces women's shoes up to a size 42 (UK 8/8½). *Passeig de Gràcia 2–4 | metro L1, L3: Pl. Catalunya | Eixample | ⎕ J8; store C/ de València 249 | metro L2, L3, L4: Passeig de Gràcia | Eixample | ⎕ J8*

34 LA MANUAL ALPARGATERA ★

The popular *espardenyes*, linen shoes with rope soles, have been made to measure in this down-to-earth family business for many generations. Whether for drop-in customers or for VIP feet such as those of Hollywood actor Michael Douglas, almost all the materials are sustainable and can be recycled. And they will fit in any suitcase! *C/ Avinyó 7 | metro L3: Liceu | Barri Gòtic | ⎕ c3*

35 VIALIS

Fine, supple materials, modern design and fair prices: once you've slipped a pair of the Barcelonian-brand Vialis onto your feet you're likely to become a repeat offender. The makers avoid artificial pigments and the shoes are produced in Spain. Several shops. *C/ Verdi 39 | metro L3: Fontana | Gràcia | ⎕ K6; C/ Elisabets 20 | metro L3: Liceu | Raval | ⎕ H9; C/ Rambla de Catalunya 86 | metro L3/L5: Diagonal | Eixample | ⎕ J8*

Camper store

NIGHTLIFE

Starry evenings for night owls: from taverns to dance halls, techno clubs to concert halls, elegant or rustic, eccentric or cosy, chintzy or post-modern. Whatever your preference, Barcelona's nightlife offers something for you.

The Santa Caterina neighbourhood is witnessing the birth of a new scene with trendy venues, especially around the market hall and the atmospheric Carrer de l'Allada-Vermell. The Gràcia quarter has an alternative vibe, with countless small pubs and bars with terraces. In summer many squares turn into open-air stages for musicians or jugglers.

You'll find all the venues in this chapter on the pull-out map ▥

Skybar at the Grand Hotel Central

Between the long-established bars and small cafés in Poble Sec a number of cult bars have set up shop off the beaten tourist track – particularly around the Carrer Blai. The Zona Alta (Upper Town) around Diagonal, Mariano Cubí and Tibidabo is the stomping ground of the fashion- and career-conscious. In summer, many hotels open their roof terraces as bars and lounges. The terraces of the fancy Pulitzer hotel, the Majestic or Grand Hotel Central are particularly beautiful. From the terraces of the hip W Hotel you have a fantastic view of the sea. One word of warning: be on your guard in the Old Town: leave your valuables at home!

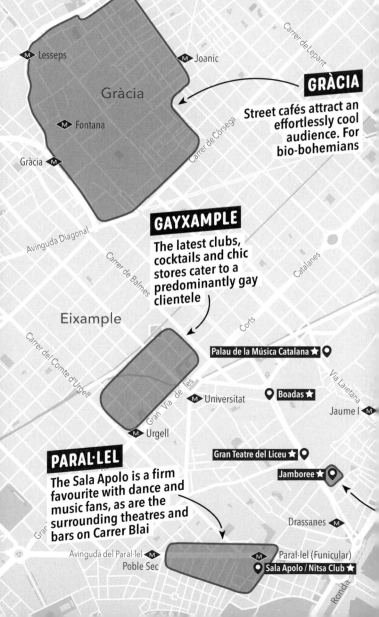

WHERE TO GO OUT IN BARCELONA

M Lesseps

M Joanic

Gràcia

M Fontana

Gràcia **M**

Carrer de Lepant

Carrer de Còrsega

GRÀCIA

Street cafés attract an effortlessly cool audience. For bio-bohemians

Avinguda Diagonal

Carrer de Balmes

GAYXAMPLE

The latest clubs, cocktails and chic stores cater to a predominantly gay clientele

Eixample

Catalanes

Carrer del Comte d'Urgell

Gran Via de les

Corts

M Universitat

Palau de la Música Catalana ★ 〇

Via Laietana

○ Boadas ★

Jaume I **M**

M Urgell

PARAL·LEL

The Sala Apolo is a firm favourite with dance and music fans, as are the surrounding theatres and bars on Carrer Blai

Gran Teatre del Liceu ★ 〇

Jamboree ★ 〇

Drassanes **M**

Avinguda del Paral·lel **M**

Poble Sec

Gran

M Paral·lel (Funicular)

○ Sala Apolo / Nitsa Club ★

Ronda

Sant Martí

SALA RAZZMATAZZ
Mega-club with five halls in former gritty, industrial Poblenou

Ⓜ Bogatell

MERCAT DEL BORN
Cool cocktail clubs, winsome wine bars and terrific tapas

🚆 Ronda

Ⓜ Barceloneta

PLAÇA REIAL
Jazz, flamenco and karaoke clubs: no.1 is Ocaña

MARCO POLO HIGHLIGHTS

★ **BOADAS**
In Hemingway's footsteps: Barcelona's legendary cocktail bar ➤ p. 98

★ **JAMBOREE**
Best jazz cellar in town ➤ p. 103

★ **SALA APOLO/NITSA CLUB**
Trendy club in a former ballroom ➤ p. 105

★ **GRAN TEATRE DEL LICEU**
More than just an opera house, it's a symbol of Catalan culture ➤ p. 107

★ **PALAU DE LA MÚSICA CATALANA**
Splendid concert hall in Art Nouveau style ➤ p. 107

400 m
437 yd

BARS & LOUNGES

1 BALIUS

It's establishments like this that give Poblenou its buzz. Behind the large shop windows of a former chemist, bartenders professionally juggle Bunsen burners and soda makers, while performers play relaxed jazz on the small stage against a delightfully retro-chic interior. *Closed Mon | C/ Pujades 196 | tel. 933 158 650 | baliusbar.com | metro L4: Poblenou | Poblenou | ▭ N 10*

2 BAR CALDERS

The ideal starting point for a pub crawl through the buzzing quarter of Sant Antoni. A home-made vermouth accompanied by some delicious pickles and served in the attractive inner courtyard will stand you in good stead for the night ahead. *Mon–Fri from 5pm, Sat/Sun from 11am | C/ del Parlament 25 | tel. 933 299 349 | FB: Bar Calders | metro L3: Poble Sec | Sant Antoni | ▭ G9*

WHERE TO START?

Nights in Barcelona start later than they do in northern Europe. For a start, dinner is eaten much later! Without wanting to sound preachy, one of the secrets to the Mediterranean nightlife is a well-filled stomach, which helps avoid any embarrassing alcohol-fuelled excesses. So, start the night in one of the many tapas bars around the **Mercat del Born** *(▭ d3)*. From here, the best cocktail bars are only a stone's throw away.

3 BIER CAB

A popular craft beer pub in the heart of "Beerxample", the brewing stronghold in the district of Eixample. With 30 draught beers, this is the perfect place to come for some home-brewed ales. The friendly bartenders will be happy to let you sample a couple of beers before you order, and you can also get burgers and other snacks to go with your drink. Also suitable for groups. *Mon–Thu noon–midnight, Fri/Sat noon–2am, Sun from 5pm | C/ Muntaner 55 | tel. 644 689 045 | biercab.com | metro L1, L2: Muntane | Eixample | ▭ H8*

4 BOADAS ★

This legendary cocktail bar is the oldest in Barcelona and with its dusty charm is still a legend; Ernest Hemingway, no less, drank his mojito here. *Mon–Sat noon–2am | C/ dels Tallers 1 | tel. 933 189 592 | boadas cocktails.com | metro: L1, L3: Catalunya | Raval | ▭ b2*

5 BOCA CHICA

The favourite hangout of choice for the young, rich and beautiful. A cocktail bar with decor that includes a wall of mirrors, Moorish tiling and American leather sofas. *Sun–Wed 5pm–1.30am, Thu–Sat 5pm–2.30am | Passatge de la Concepció 12 | tel. 934 675 149 | bocagrande.cat/en/boca-chica | metro L4, L5: Diagonal | Eixample | ▭ J7*

A freshly mixed cocktail at Boca Chica, ready to be savoured on the leather sofas

6 CANIGÓ

For those who have seen enough super-styled lounges in Barcelona and would like to know what an authentic Catalan bar looks like, this is the right place. In the evenings, this traditional bar in the Gràcia neighbourhood is often jam-packed and noisy, even without the music. Good value. *Mon–Thu 10am–2am, Fri 10am–3am, Sat 8pm–3am | C/ de Verdi 2 | tel. 932 133 049 | barcanigo.com | metro L3: Fontana | Gràcia | ⸫ J6*

7 CHATELET

This could be the living room of a cutting-edge designer and flea market freak – it's one of the most popular bars in Gràcia. Cocktails ordered before 10pm only cost 4 euros. *Daily 6pm–2.30am | C/ Torrijos 54 | FB: Chatelet Bar | metro L3: Fontana | Gràcia | ⸫ K6*

8 CHICHA LIMONÀ

Generous pavements full of tables and chairs with mighty plane trees for shade: it's no wonder that Passeig Sant Joan is fast becoming Barcelona's new favourite promenade. Add to that creative restaurateurs who find the perfect balance between originality and quality with a sense of community, and there's nothing standing in the way of a relaxed summer evening. The best example on the square: this vermouth bar in true recycling-chic glory. The cocktail menu is fit for a movie with creations like *Lost in Translation* (gin with cherry liqueur and elderberry juice)! *Tue–Thu 9.30am–1pm, Fri/Sat 9.30am–2pm, Sun 9.30am–5pm | Passeig de Sant Joan 80 | tel. 932 776 403 | chichalimona.com | metro 4: Girona | Eixample | ⸫ K8*

INSIDER TIP
Toast in scarlet

A glittering journey back in time at El Nacional – cava and oysters included

9 BUENAS TARDES PULITZER

The city is, quite literally, at the feet of this lounge! Located near Plaça de Catalunya, it was one of the first to allow non-guests up on its roof and has been a nightlife staple ever since. Enjoy cocktails and concerts on the rooftop from May to October. *Wed–Sun 5-11pm | C/ Bergara 8 | tel. 934 816 767 | hotelpulitzer.es | metro L1, L3: Pl. Catalunya | Rambla | ▱ b1*

10 PARADISO

Served at a curved wooden counter, the cocktails here will make you question the laws of nature. The Space Colada glows like a spaceship in outer space, while the Volcano Negroni looks as if it's actually spewing lava. The cocktail bar has even been named the third best in the world for its top-notch recipes. Waiting a few minutes outside the door is all part of the experience. *Mon-Thu 6pm-midnight, Fri–Sun 5pm-midnight | C/ Rera Palau 4 | paradiso.cat | metro L4: Barceloneta | Ribera | ▱ d4*

11 EL MAMA Y LA PAPA

Warning: you might struggle to concentrate here. After all, what do you focus your attention on first – the artist on the trapeze or the temptingly fragrant Asian chicken on the plate? It's a difficult conundrum! The food in this huge industrial loft is as exquisite as the entertainment. No wonder: Álvaro Garcés, the chef at the gastro-cabaret, learned from three-star chef Martín Berasategui. *Thu 7pm-2.30am, Sat/Sun 7pm-3am | Passatge Pere Calders 2 | tel. 934 417 662 | elmama. barcelona | metro L3: Poble Sec | Sant Antoni | ▱ G10*

12 EL NACIONAL

As soon as you get through the door you may well find yourself carried away by the Charleston rhythms that play here, as this palace of bling is a unique homage to the roaring twenties. Inside the enormous hall – previously a car park – you can shimmy your way between four different bars and four restaurant areas that will easily keep you occupied for an entire evening, but make sure to dress well. First up is the oyster bar – nowhere does cava taste better! *Sun–Wed noon–2am, Thu–Sat noon–3am | Passeig de Gràcia 24 | tel. 935 185 053 | elnacionalbcn.com | metro L2, L4: Passeig de Gràcia | Eixample | ⌑ c1*

INSIDER TIP
Bubbly twenties style

13 GRAN BODEGA SALTÓ

Creative, kitschy and cosy – the curious decoration of the more than 100-year-old bodega was created by a local artist. Likeable corner bar and cultural meeting point, on many days with live music. The proceeds go towards neighbourly help in the Poble Sec quarter. *Mon–Wed 7pm–2am, Thu–Sun noon–3am | Blesa 36 | tel. 934 413 709 | bodega salto.net | metro L2, L3: Paral·lel | Poble Sec | ⌑ G10*

14 L'ENTRESÒL

A trendy cocktail and music bar in the Gràcia quarter for Barcelona's night owls, stylish in black, red and white. Dim light, selected drinks and excellent gin and tonics. *Wed–Sat from 8pm | Planeta 39 | tel. 685 533 941 | lentresol.negocio.site | metro L3: Fontana | Gràcia | ⌑ J6*

15 LONDON BAR

This bohemian bar with its listed Art Nouveau counter has become a staple in the Raval quarter. Don't be surprised if someone performs tricks on the trapeze or ladies in glittery costumes perform backflips in the backroom: the Catalan circus family Raluy runs the show at the London Bar. *Sun–Fri 5pm–2.30am, Thu, Sun live music from 11pm, Fri/Sat 7am–3am | C/ Nou de la Rambla 34 | tel. 938 082 187 | londonbar-bar.nego cio.site | metro L3: Liceu | Raval | ⌑ b3*

16 MIRABÉ

Aperitifs, long drinks – and a breathtaking view across the whole of Barcelona. In the summer there's a garden terrace. *Tue from 6.30pm, Wed–Sun from 12.30pm | C/ de Manuel Arnús 2 | tel. 934 185 880 | mirabe.com | FGC: Tibidabo, change to Tramvía Blau or bus no. 196 | Sarrià-Sant Gervasi | ⌑ J2*

17 CASA MORITZ

Barcelona's favourite beer brews here in copper kettles before being freshly tapped. Tapas are served at industrial-chic bars and tables. *Sun–Thu noon–1am, Fri/Sat noon–2am | Ronda de Sant Antoni 41 | fabricamoritz barcelona.com | metro L1, L2: Universitat | Sant Antoni | ⌑ J8*

18 SOLANGE

This bar is named after the Bond girl from *Casino Royale*, and that's not the only inspiration it draws from the 007 films, with its elegant bar, vintage sofas and – of course – vodka martinis. The Pernías family who run the place insist on classic chic, so you won't find any novelty flowers or cocktail umbrellas here. *Daily 6pm–2.30am | C/ d'Aribau 143 | tel. 931 643 625 | solangecocktail.com | metro L5: Hospital Clinic | Eixample | ⊞ H7*

19 MARIPOSA NEGRA

This cocktail bar's interior designers could well have been inspired by filmmaker Tim Burton, and much of the bar is straight out of a fantasy world. The prototypes for the, well, containers (for want of a better word) from which the creations are sampled are 3D printed before being made, fired and painted in the in-house ceramics studio. Make sure to try the signature drink *Melancólico* with rum, home-

made orange liqueur and tiger-nut milk. *Daily 1pm–2am | Pl. de les Olles 4 | tel. 671 619 762 | mariposa negrabar.com | metro L4: Jaume I | Ribera | ⊞ d4*

20 TWO SCHMUCKS

Founded by Norwegian globetrotter Moe Aljaff, Two Schmucks is one of the few establishments in Barcelona able to sustain itself without outside backers or hospitality groups behind it. From the steel staircase to the whitewashed walls – absolutely everything is done in-house and it is much revered as a result! *Daily 6pm–2am | C/ de Joaquín Costa 52 | tel. 634 651 000 | twoschmucks.com | metro L1, L2: Universitat | El Raval | ⊞ a1*

> **INSIDER TIP**
> **DIY meets steel art**

Dance till dawn: in the hip clubs a lot is going on

21 4 LATAS

Wine and vermouth bars often play on nostalgic charm. But this bar in Eixample proves modern, light venues are just as well suited to the classic Spanish aperitif wine. Behind the large glass front, a mixed crowd starts their evening with tapas and the slightly oily fortified wine. Excellent wine list. *Mon-Wed noon-1am, Thu noon-2am, Fri/Sat noon-3am, Sun 6pm-midnight | C/ Muntaner 211 | tel. 931 893 122 | 4latas.com | metro L5: Hospital Clínic | Eixample | ⌂ H7*

DISCOS, CLUBS & LIVE MUSIC

22 ANTILLA BARCELONA

One of the leading salsa clubs, where immigrants from the Caribbean dance their homesickness away. *Wed-Sat from 11pm, Sun from 7pm | C/ d'Aragó 141 | antillasalsa.com | metro L5: Hospital Clínic | Eixample | ⌂ G8*

23 DIOBAR

Tango, Afrobeats, reggae, Brazilian – whatever the dance craze, this small basement bar under Barcelona's flagship Greek eatery at Ciutadella Park has become a classic in the city's nightlife – and the prices aren't bad either. *Wed-Sat from 10pm, Sun from 9.30pm | Av. del Marquès de l'Argentera 27 | dionisosrestaurants.com/en/diobar | admission 3-5 euros | metro L4: Barceloneta | El Born | ⌂ d4*

24 ELROW

Strictly speaking, this open-air party temple is not part of Barcelona proper. But once you've made the journey to the suburbs and spent the night dancing among beauties in feather boas and breathtakingly high platform shoes, the stars shining bright above you, booming bass reverberating through your bones and glitter confetti from the giant cannon falling all around you, you'll want to come back. *See website for opening hours and shows | C31, Km186.1 (at Viladecans) | tel. 638 836 321 | elrow.com | metro L1: Espanya, then by bus L94 | Viladecans | ⌂ c9*

25 JAMBOREE ★

Back in the day, stars such as Dexter Gordon and Ornette Coleman performed in the legendary jazz cellar. International guests still perform and there's a dance floor. *Live music Tue-Sun 8 and 10pm, Mon only 8pm, disco from midnight | Plaça Reial 17 | masimas.com | metro L3: Liceu | Barri Gòtic | ⌂ b3*

26 JAZZSÍ CLUB TALLER DE MÚSICS

You may not recognize the name of the jazz performer on the bill, but don't worry, you will in the future. The small club has become a rehearsal space for the famous music school. Who knows, you could be watching the next Amy Winehouse or Chet Baker! 🐷 At 8-10 euros including a drink, admission to see the stars of tomorrow is a bargain, with something for everyone on the programme. *Mon jazz, Thu/Sun rock & blues, Wed jam session, Thu Cuban music, Fri/Sat flamenco, varying opening times, see*

Night flows into day at Opium beach club

website | C/ Requesens 2 | tel. 933 290 020 | tallerdemusics.com | metro L2: Sant Antoni | Raval | ⊞ a2

27 MACARENA CLUB

Don't come here if you value your personal space: the dancefloor is only a few metres wide, though to the DJs who perform here it might as well be a superclub. Fans of house and minimal techno swear by the line-up. *Sun–Thu midnight–5am, Fri/Sat midnight–6am | C/ Nou de Sant Francesc 5 | macarena club.com | metro L3: Drassanes | Barri Gòtic | ⊞ b3*

28 MARULA CAFÉ

Black music, soul, funk, house, hip-hop, DJ sessions. *Mon–Sat from 11pm | C/ dels Escudellers 49 | marula.cafe. com | metro L3: Drassanes | Barri Gòtic | ⊞ b3*

29 MOOG

Excellent music programme with well-known DJs. Cellar club for lovers of techno and electronic music. *Daily from midnight | C/ de l'Arc del Teatre 3 | masimas.com | metro L3: Liceu | Raval | ⊞ b3*

30 OPIUM

Out with flip-flops and in with high heels: at this beach club you can find a crowd of French, British and American guests dressed to the nines on the packed-out dancefloor. It's the beach club of choice for professional party-goers, not least due to the incredible light show. Also has a restaurant. *Daily noon–6am | Passeig Marítim 34 | opiumbarcelona.com | metro L4: Ciutadella Vila Olímpica | La Barceloneta | ⊞ L11*

31 OTTO ZUTZ CLUB

Popular industrial-look club spanning three floors. DJ sessions, electronic, reggaeton, hip-hop. Things only get going around 2am. *Wed–Sun from midnight | C/ de Lincoln 15 | ottozutz. com | FGC: Gràcia | metro L3: Fontana | Sant Gervasi | ☐ H6*

32 SALA APOLO/NITSA CLUB ★

This elegant former ballroom has been a staple of Barcelona's nightlife since its inception. Where couples used to dance the polka, today bodies thrash to rhythms of all kinds at the Nitsa Club. From electro rock to disco pop and electronic experiments: every style has its day of the week. The live music calendar is also well worth a look! *C/ de Nou de la Rambla 113 | tel. 934 414 001 | sala-apolo.com | metro L3: Parallel | Poble Sec | ☐ a3*

33 SALA BECOOL

Downstairs you'll find revellers raving to electronic music, while upstairs the playlist includes indie, pop and rock. These two very different worlds are brought together by some extremely hip haircuts and a casual atmosphere. That might also explain why the club owners opted for a revolving dance-floor: that way, the partygoers can show themselves off on all sides without forgoing an ounce of coolness. The crowd is aged 20 and up. *Fri–Sun midnight–6am | Plaça Joan Llongueras 5 | salabecool.com | metro L5: Hospital Clinic | Galvany | ☐ G6*

34 SALA RAZZMATAZZ

One of Barcelona's trendiest mega clubs, situated in an old industrial building of Poblenou, with five different floors and current music styles. Well-known bands such as Coldplay and Kraftwerk have performed here. *Wed–Sat, opening times and concerts vary, see website | Pamplona 88 | tel. 933 208 200 | salarazzmatazz.com | metro L4: Bogatell oder Marina | Sant Martí | ☐ M10*

35 SIDECAR FACTORY CLUB

Cult basement club on Plaça Reial. Since 1982, this veritable institution has shown a flair for finding musicians with their finger on the pulse without jumping on every latest trend. The tube-shaped venue under Plaça Reial is full of an enthusiastic crowd celebrating DJs and bands from the underground scene. From rock and pop to soul and electronic music. To top it off, the club hosts photo, poster and design exhibitions. *Wed–Sat from 6pm | Plaça Reial 7 | tel. 933 021 586 | sidecar.es | metro L3: Drassanes | Barri Gòtic | ⊞ b3*

36 ROUGE

The red velvet curtain and long corridor convey a touch of the David Lynch, the cocktails are top-notch, and the DJ sets are bang on trend. The venue is a firm favourite with the cultural elite and is an ideal choice for a nightcap after a trip to the theatre or a musical at Paral·lel. *Wed, Thu, Sun 7pm–1am, Fri/Sat 7pm–3am | C/ Poeta Cabanyes 21 | Instagram: @rouge_barcelona | metro L2: Paral·lel | Poble Sec | ⊞ G10*

FLAMENCO

37 PALAU DALMASES / ESPAI BARROC

The ambience alone is spectacular: the Palau Dalmases is one of the Old Town's most beautiful Baroque palaces. Of an evening, when the heels on the small stage clap to the atmospheric candlelight, a concert becomes a real experience. *Flamenco concerts daily at 6, 7.15, 8.15 and 9.15pm | admission from 25 euros | C/ Montcada 20 | tel. 660 769 865 | flamenco palaudalmases.com | metro L4: Jaume I | El Born | ⊞ d3*

38 TABLAO DE CARMEN

Where the Tablao de Carmen stands today, the legendary flamenco dancer Carmen Amaya debuted for the opening of the World Exhibition in 1929. Authentic flamenco and a programme for the discerning, in the Poble Espanyol museum village. Wine and dinner round off any authentic experience. *Performances daily 6pm (show starts 6.40pm) and 8.30pm (show starts 9.15pm) | admission 45 euros incl. drink and admission to Poble Espanyol, 63 euros with tapas menu | tel. 933 256 895 | tablaode carmen.com | metro L1, L3: Espanya, onwards on foot or by bus 61, 13: Poble Espanyol | Montjuïc | ⊞ E9*

39 TARANTOS

Many great names of flamenco have performed here in the city's oldest *tablao*, from Antonio Gades to Duquende. *Daily live flamenco at 6.30, 7.30, 8.30pm | admission for a flamenco show from 17 euros | Plaça Reial 17 | tel. 933 191 789 | tarantosbarcelona. com | metro L3: Liceu | Barri Gòtic | ⊞ b3*

40 23 ROBADOR

A flashing number 23 lights the way to this club and simultaneously signals the fact that this area doesn't have the best reputation, with the red-light district starting just down the road. But don't be put off, as you'll miss out on the best flamenco bar in the city. This cosy 20m² bar hosts performances by Andalusian and Catalonian stars, all lapped up by an enthusiastically clapping audience. It was in dives like this that flamenco first developed, long before it achieved its current popularity and moved to more salubrious establishments. So really, this is the real deal! *Daily 7pm–2.30am |*

INSIDER TIP
A cult dive

C/ d'en Robador 23 | 23robadors.com | metro L3: Liceu | El Raval | ▥ b3

CONCERT HALLS & OPERA

🔢 AUDITORI DE BARCELONA (AUDITORIUM)

Designed by Rafael Moneo and inaugurated in 1999, the building next to the national theatre is the modern heart of concert life. Top international stars perform in the auditorium, and the symphony orchestra is also based here. *C/ de Lepant 150 | tel. 932 479 300 | auditori.com | metro L1: Glòries, L2: Monumental | Eixample | ▥ L9*

🔢 GRAN TEATRE DEL LICEU ⭐

When the historic theatre on La Rambla burnt down in 1994, the flames not only destroyed one of Europe's most beautiful opera houses: the Liceu most of all symbolised the Catalans' self-confidence and culture, as a counterpoint to Madrid. While the auditorium has risen again in its old splendour, the stage is now amongst the world's most modern. Artistically too, this temple to the muses has been dusted down, with contemporary works and modern musical theatre alongside the traditional repertoire. *La Rambla 51–59 | tel. 934 859 913 | liceubarcelona.cat | metro L3: Liceu | El Raval | ▥ b3*

🔢 PALAU DE LA MÚSICA CATALANA ⭐

Although the Art Nouveau splendour in this concert hall makes it difficult to concentrate on the music, the

A feast for eyes and ears at the Palau de la Música Catalana

programme merits your undivided attention. Every year, over 200 concerts take place here, including international star performances – from classical and jazz to chanson or world music. 👥 At family concerts, even the little ones can have fun; search *"conciertos familiars"* on the website's homepage. *C/ Palau de la Música 4–6 | tel. 932 957 200 | palaumusica.cat | metro L1, L4: Urquinaona | Sant Pere | ▥ c2*

ACTIVE & RELAXED

Take a break on the bright tiled benches in Park Güell

SPORT & WELLNESS

CYCLING

Gone are the days when cycling through Barcelona included a death-defying dance amid hordes of humming Vespas and honking cars – and thank goodness for that! With over 300km of safe, well-developed bike paths, the Mediterranean metropolis is now well on its way to becoming one of Southern Europe's cycling cities. Fortunately for tourists, shared mobility providers have also grown wise to this! Companies like *Donkey-Bike (donkey.bike, around 2.50 euros/2 hrs)* have scattered their bikes city-wide. You just need to sign up, search the app for the closest free bike and start cycling. Then just park it again once you're done. Not only are bikes the fastest mode of transport to the Sagrada Família and the like, they also make it easy to climb the local mountains Montjuïc and Tibidabo: e-bikes are now standard!

DANCING

Tango? Salsa? Or do you prefer swing? The *Glorieta (metro L1: Arc de Triomf | ▥ K10)* pavilion next to the monumental fountain in the Parc de la Ciutadella is taken over by the city's dance enthusiasts. On Wednesdays, the dance floor is filled with the eight beats of the tango, and Sundays are for salsa fans to swing their hips, while other days are set aside for Lindy Hop fans to twirl through the air. 🐷 Newcomers are often treated to a free dance lesson before the start. Portable loudspeakers cater for the music. Days and times can vary, but more info is available at *tangoenbarcelona.es* or *bcnswing.org*.

INSIDER TIP
Free lessons for beginners?

FOOTBALL ▸

Last-minute ticket for the big *clásico* when Real Madrid face FC Barcelona?

Sports in Barcelona – you'll be spoiled for choice with options in all corners of the city

No chance. The whole city is on its feet when Catalonia's star club takes on its arch-rival from the locally unpopular Spanish capital, because Barça is so much *més que un club* (more than a club) – it's the ultimate symbol of Catalan pride. The enormous stadium ★ *Camp Nou* is well worth seeing. But if you're hoping to see Ansu Fati in red and blue, you need to snap up tickets well in advance. Online sales begin around a month in advance and tickets can also be bought by phone around a fortnight before the match. All sold out? Don't be too disappointed. You can watch the team's feats on screen in the huge *football museum (April–Sept daily 9.30am–7pm, Oct–March Mon–Sat 10am–6.30pm, Sun 10am–2.30pm, times may vary on match days! | admission to the museum and stadium tour 28 euros | Aristides Maillol | tel. 934 963 600 | fcbarcelona.com |* *metro L5: Collblanc or L3: Maria Cristina | ▭ D6).* Fans can pose adoringly in front of the impressive collection of trophies this top club, founded in 1899, has won, while the stadium tour even offers a chance to walk through the players' tunnel. Goosebumps guaranteed!

INLINE SKATING

It's hardly surprising that in Barcelona it feels as if half the city is on skates. The promenades along the coast and around the Parc de la Ciutadella are wide and mostly tiled, with mile after mile of bike paths added in recent years. In other words, it's perfect for rollerbladers! Small groups of inline skaters often of cruise through the city, covering 12 different routes. Head to the Facebook page of skating club *Patinar BCN* for more info.

If you don't want to take part, you can watch seasoned skaters showcase their skills on Tuesdays and Sundays – for free, of course (Tue 9pm, Sun 7pm, winter 5pm | meeting point Paseo García Farias on the corner of Lope de Vega and Espronceda | metro L4: Poblenou | Poblenou | ⌨ O11).

If you didn't have space in your suitcase to pack your skates, you can rent a pair at *RSB Rental Scooter Barcelona (top floor of the El Centre de la Vila shopping centre) (rollerblades 5 euros/hr, 15 euros/day, 50 euros/ week | Carrer de Salvador Espriu 63 | tel. 640 559 468 | rentalscooter barcelona.com | metro: L4 Ciutadela/ Vila Olímpica | ⌨ M11).*

SPORT ON THE BEACH

Four kilometres of beach under an almost permanently blue sky: it doesn't take long for the mind to drift to sport. At Barceloneta, yogis greet the sun together every morning. If you fancy joining, you can find English-speaking groups on *meetup.com*.

And if your biceps are in need of some toning, but you're not in the mood for a stuffy gym, then head to the beach! The city executive must have had the body-conscious in mind during Barceloneta's all-round make-over, installing pull-up bars, wall bars, ab trainers and other fitness equipment along the promenade. Plus, they're free of charge and usable all year round! *(e.g. Passeig Marítim de la Barceloneta 17 | metro L4: Ciutadella | ⌨ K12).* If you prefer to train with a coach, you can book an hour of beach *fitness* with Mark Castley and Andy

Roberts *(Mon–Sat | tel. 673 223 946 | beachfitbcn@gmail.com | meeting point: Plaça del Mar | FB: Beachfitbcn | metro L4: Barceloneta | ⌨ J12).* Developed by two North Americans, the programme combines endurance with strength. People come together to sweat it out together.

STAND-UP PADDLEBOARDING

Surfers may well turn their noses up at paddleboarding but, for a start, there are rarely any waves big enough to surf in the Med, and anyway, it's great fun to balance on the water with a paddle in your hand. The seas are calm, and with the right supervision, it's really not that hard. So give it a go! Water babies can learn to paddle at the *Moloka'i SUP Center (2-hr private course 40 euros, 90-min group session 20 euros | C/ de Meer 39 | tel. 654 082 099 | molokaisupcenter.com | ⌨ K12).*

SWIMMING & SPAS

Escape the city noise and head to the subterranean baths of the ☂ *Aire de Barcelona (Mon–Thu 9am–10pm, Fri 9am–11pm, Sat/Sun 8am–11pm | incl. aromatherapy from 60 euros; incl. half-hour massage from 95 euros | online booking only | Passeig de Picasso 22 | tel. 932 955 743 | beaire. com | metro L1: Arc de Triomf | ⌨ K10)* at Parc de la Ciutadella. The lights are dimmed as you float, just as the Romans once did, under the impressive, vaulted ceilings in pools of different temperatures. Or you can sip tea on warm stone benches. And if you still can't forget your everyday worries, the professional massage team is

After a workout on the beach, the sea is the perfect place to cool off

guaranteed to knead away any remaining tension.

The futuristic design of the three bathing capsules in the *Flotarium (Mon–Sat noon–9pm | single session 50 mins 40 euros | Plaça Narcís Oller 3 | flotarium.com | Metro L3, L5: Diagonal | ▥ J7)* is no coincidence. Once inside the tank, you will feel as weightless as an astronaut floating through space. The salt content is matched to that of the Dead Sea, the water temperature to your own body. Total relaxation guaranteed!

At *Le Patio Spa (Mon–Sat 10am–8pm, Sun 11am–8pm | facials from 45, hammam from 35 euros | C/ Compte d'Urgell 107 | tel. 935 256 700 | lepatiospa.com | metro L1: Urgell, L5: Hospital Clínic | ▥ G8)* you can your muscles in the bubble pool and hammam, then allow a professional beautician to pamper you, before finally unwinding on the whitewashed, landscaped patio. The spa in Eixample combines French *savoir-vivre* with professional expertise, but still remains affordable.

FESTIVALS & EVENTS

JANUARY
Cavalcada de Reis Magnificent procession of the Three Wise Men through the city centre on 5 January.

MARCH
International vintage car rally Rally between Barcelona and Sitges. *Tel. 938 949 357 | rallyesitges.com*

Marató Barcelona Popular marathon run on the second Sunday in March. Start and finish: Plaça de Espanya. Booking up to 24 hours before the start. *Tel. 902 431 763 | barcelona marato.es*

APRIL
⭐ **Sant Jordi (Day of the Book)** In honour of Saint George, patron saint of Catalonia, people give each other a red rose. Books are sold on streets and squares, 10% cheaper than usual. If you're happy to wait in line, you might well manage to snare an autograph from your favourite author. *23 April*

MAY
Saló Internacional del Còmic Major international comic fair. *Mid-May | comic-barcelona.com*

JUNE
Sonar (International Festival of Advanced Music and Multimedia Arts) International techno and electric music. At the fringe festival, Sonar+D, sound researchers and artists present new developments from the world of digital wonders. *Mid-June*

⭐ **Nit de Sant Joan** The whole city celebrates the shortest night of the year with jumps over bonfires and a big fireworks display. *23/24 June*

Primavera Sound One of the largest indie rock festivals in Europe. *prima vera sound.com*

The *gegants*, or giants, add to the fun on Barcelona's streets

JULY/AUGUST

Grec International arts festival with concerts, spoken word and dance, featuring stars as well as interesting newcomers. *lameva.barcelona.cat/grec*

Festa Major de Gràcia The streets and squares of Gràcia are covered in spectacular decorations for Barcelona's most popular neighbourhood festival. There are concerts and dance performances, theatre and processions, as well as street artists and activities for children. The neighbours put tables and chairs out in front of their houses, rivers of wine and beer flow. *festamajordegracia.cat*

SEPTEMBER

⭐ **Festa de la Mercè** Popular feast honouring Barcelona's patron saint in the days around 24 Sept. Experience 🚩 *castells* (human towers), and head to the Seguici, the procession of the *gegants* (giant figures), fire-spewing dragons and dancing devils. *bcn.es/merce*

INSIDER TIP
Diabolical fun

Barcelona Acció Musical (BAM) The festival for alternative music styles is held at the same time as the Festa de la Mercè. Free admission. *bcn.es/bam*

OCTOBER–DECEMBER

International Jazz Festival An institution: concerts are held at different performance venues. *theproject.es*

DECEMBER

Fira de Santa Llúcia Nativity and Christmas market with magical stalls around Advent time in front of the Gothic cathedral. *firadesantallucia.cat*

SLEEP WELL

SHOE COMFORT

If you're tired, chill in the hammock! If you're hungry, head to the lobby fridge for fresh yoghurt, fruit or salmon sandwiches. Life at *Casa Camper (40 rooms | C/ d'Elisabets 11 | tel. 933 426 280 | casacamper.com | metro L1, L3: Catalunya | €€€ | El Raval | ⌘ b2)* is as relaxed and comfortable as the shoes of the same name. Plus, it's right at the heart of the Old Town, and just a stone's throw away from the Mallorcan shoe brand's nearest store.

BEHIND GOTHIC WALLS

If you fancy a trip back in time, this is the place for you. The oldest stones that make up the hotel ★ *Mercer (28 rooms | C/ dels Lledó 7 | tel. 933 107 480 | mercerbarcelona.com | metro L1: Jaume I | €€€ | Barri Gòtic | ⌘ c2)* date back to Roman times, while the two watchtowers on the roof terrace were once part of the city wall. As

for the rest? Timeless elegance and luxury.

METROPOLITAN RETREAT FOR WINE LOVERS

Top-quality finish, stylish urban design and lasting memories: a match made in heaven. If you love good wine, you will love the *Praktik Vinoteca (64 rooms | C/ Balmes 51 | tel. 934 545 028 | hotelpraktikvinoteca.com | metro L1: Universitat | €€ | Eixample | ⌘ H8)*! On arrival, the sommelier will greet you with a complimentary glass of wine, while afternoons are for guests to talk shop over tastings on the lounge bar's expansive leather sofas. The rooms might be on the small side but are comfortable and very much in keeping with the wine theme. Cheers!

HOME FROM HOME

Wake up and start your day with sun salutations on the balcony (there are

yoga mats by every bed), and a cappuccino from Barcelona's best barista. Then browse the hotel's book and shirt shop for unique local designs. *Casa Bonay (67 rooms | Gran Via de les Corts Catalanes 700 | tel. 935 458 050 | casabonay.com | metro L2: Tetuán | €€ | Eixample | ⊞ d1)* is a home from home for international hipsters, which is exactly why it's 100% Barcelona. Even if you don't stay here, you are still welcome to enjoy the great view, fragrant herb garden and delicious tapas on the roof terrace!

INSIDER TIP
Hipsters on the roof!

HOME FOR A WHILE
So excited by Barcelona you dream of moving here? *The5rooms (12 rooms, 2 apartments | C/ Pau Claris 72 | tel. 933 427 880 | the5rooms.com | metro L1: Urquinaona | €€ | Eixample | ⊞ c1)* is a great place to test the waters. You'll feel right at home at the large breakfast table in the apartment, which has been converted into an upmarket guesthouse. There were originally only five rooms but luckily this option in elegant Eixample has been expanded.

COLOUR AT THE TOUCH OF A BUTTON
Feeling blue? Simply push a button, and the white walls of your room will change colour to match. If you are stuck in your room on a rainy day, then why not turn everything bright yellow? The smart, cleverly LED-illuminated hotel ★ *Chic&Basic Born (31 rooms | C/ de la Princesa 50 | tel. 932 954 652 | chicandbasic.com | metro L1: Arc de Triomf | €€ | El Born | ⊞ d3)* allows the otherwise white rooms to glow in whatever colour takes your fancy. The shower in the middle of the room throws convention to the wind, as is the wont with avant-garde hotels!

DISCOVERY TOURS

Do you want to get under the skin of the city? Then these discovery tours provide the perfect guide. They include advice on which sights to visit, tips on where to stop for that perfect holiday snap, a choice of the best places to eat and drink and suggestions for fun activities.

Mercat de Sant Josep (La Boqueria)

Montbau

Ronda de Dalt

La Guineueta

Prosperidad

La Vall d'Hebron

Horta

Ronda de Dalt

Passeig de Valldaura

Vallcarca

Park Güell

Vila Ricina

Passeig de Maragall

1

El Carmel

Avinguda Meridiana

(Ronda del Mig) Travessera de Dalt · Ronda de

Sant Andreu

Gracia

Ronda de

Congres

Guinardo

El Camp de l'Arpa

La Sagrera

St. Marti de Provençals

Avinguda Meridiana

a Dreta l'Eixample

1

Diagonal

El Clot

La Verneda

Corts Catalanes

Autopista

Barcelona

Mataro

El Fort Pius

Poble Nou

2 A stroll through the Ribera Quarter

Parc Zoologic

Ronda Litoral

4

Sun, sea & sand

La Barceloneta

Mar Mediterrània

1 km
0.62 mi

❶ BARCELONA AT A GLANCE

➤ Mysterious Gothic: out and about in the Old Town
➤ Gaudi the great: Barcelona's famous landmarks
➤ Big-city glamour: between skaters and opera lovers

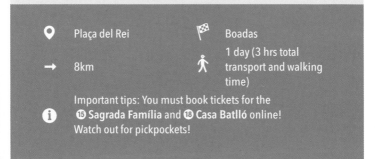

📍 Plaça del Rei

🏁 Boadas

→ 8km

🚶 1 day (3 hrs total transport and walking time)

ℹ Important tips: You must book tickets for the ⓯ **Sagrada Família** and ⓲ **Casa Batlló** online! Watch out for pickpockets!

---

❶ Plaça del Rei

❷ Museu d'Història de la Ciutat

IN THE FOOTSTEPS OF THE ROMANS

Start off from ❶ Plaça del Rei ➤ p. 30. This square with the Royal Palace, the quirky medieval watchtower and the ❷ Museu d'Història de la Ciutat ➤ p. 30 is a gem of Gothic architecture. As you pass the museum's floor-to-ceiling windows, look down on the exhibit of Roman ruins under Barcelona. *From Plaça del Rei, follow Carrer dels Comtes to Plaça de Sant Iu.* The medieval patio belonging to the Royal Palace that now houses the Museu Frederic Marès ➤ p. 31 is utterly charming. Across the way, you can glimpse the side aisle of the ❸ Catedral ➤ p. 32. This mighty cathedral's most impressive features include the beautiful choir stalls and the fascinating cloister with cackling geese.

❸ Catedral

TO THE MIDDLE AGES & BACK

❹ Plaça de Sant Felip Neri

❺ El Call

After a little detour to the idyllic, and usually crowded, old town square ❹ Plaça de Sant Felip Neri ➤ p. 32, head on to the Jewish quarter ❺ El Call. *Wander through the narrow Gothic streets of Sant Server and Sant Domènec del Call,* and pass by Barcelona's historic Synagoge on Carrer de Marlet, which bears witness to centuries of Jewish life. If you look closely, you can still spot the remains of the city wall on a house in Carrer del Call. *From Carrer del Call, go right on Banys Nous with its lovely little shops. Keep walking for a few minutes and then take the side street Carrer de l'Ave Maria to the left and stroll over the picturesque "twin squares"*, namely **❻ Plaça de Sant Josep Oriol/Plaça del Pi**, *before heading past Santa María del Pi church and walking down Carrer Cardenal Casañas towards Barcelona's famous boulevard,* **❼ La Rambla ➤ p. 46**, just a stone's throw away.

❻ Plaça de Sant Josep Oriol/Plaça del Pi

❼ La Rambla

REVEL IN ART NOUVEAU

Take a quick look at or into the Gran Teatre del Liceu (opera house) before treating yourself to something delicious at the charming Art Nouveau ❽ Pastelería Escribà ➤ p. 88. Afterwards, and with your strength restored, explore the hip district of ❾ Raval ➤ p. 46. *From La Rambla, turn down Hospital Street with its colourful bars and façades covered with paper art and head for the Gothic* ❿ Antic Hospital de la Santa Creu ➤ p. 48, where you'll be tempted to stop for a while under the orange trees of the romantic inner courtyard.

❽ Pastelería Escribà

❾ Raval

❿ Antic Hospital de la Santa Creu

GOOD ART, GOOD CULTURE, GOOD FOOD

Exit the courtyard on the other side along Carrer del Carme. Follow Carrer dels Àngels to the ⓫ Museu d'Art Contemporani ➤ p. 47. Skaters from all over Europe show off their tricks in front of the museum's gleaming white façade. Next door, the old centre of Barcelona is reflected in a spectacular glass construction on the patio of the ⓬ Centre de Cultura Contemporània ➤ p. 47. By now you've really earned a lunch break. *Take the always-lively Carrer Elisabets to return to La Rambla and walk down the boulevard a bit, heading towards the harbour, to* ⓭ Mercat de Sant Josep ➤ p. 77. Most of the stalls in the famous market hall, the "belly of Barcelona", now offer snacks and delicious treats of all kinds. If you want something warm, grab a bite to eat at El Quim de la Boqueria ➤ p. 78 with its lively atmosphere. The Kiosko Universal ➤ p. 78 is another good alternative, especially the lunch menu.

INSIDER TIP
Inside Europe's skating capital

⓫ Museu d'Art Contemporani

⓬ Centre de Cultura Contemporània

⓭ Mercat de Sant Josep

GAUDÍ TO THE POWER OF THREE

When you've finished eating, *take the metro to* ⓮ Park Güell ➤ p. 58. The panoramic view of the city from Antoni Gaudí's fantastical park is absolutely worth a visit! *Return to the metro station and continue to* Gaudi's world-famous basilica, the ⓯ Sagrada Família ➤ p. 43, which you have just admired from above. Barcelona's main landmark is an absolute must-see! Gaudí's Nativity façade and the spectacular interior of

⓮ Park Güell

⓯ Sagrada Família

A dream home with a scaly exterior: Casa Battló looks like something out of a fairy tale

the gigantic nave with its imposing columns branching upwards are particularly noteworthy. Are you ready for a break and something sweet? The traditional croissants and muffins at the bakery ⑯ Turris *(C/ Provença 485), just a few steps from the Nativity façade,* are a tasty treat. Why not take one back to the small park for one last look at Gaudí's masterpiece.

⑯ Turris

THE STARS OF MODERNISME
Catalan Art Nouveau is more than just Gaudí. Some of the most significant Art Nouveau buildings from the great masters line Barcelona's fine and fancy boulevard ⑰ Passeig de Gràcia ➤ p. 40: Casa Amatller ➤ p. 40 by Josep Puig i Cadalfalch, Casa Lleó Morera ➤ p. 40 by Lluis Domènech i Montaner, and Antoni Gaudí's wavy Casa Milà ➤ p. 42. The best way to become better acquainted with Gaudí's style is to visit the ⑱ Casa Batlló ➤ p. 41 and its quirky rooftop terrace, whose rolling form resembles a reptile.

⑰ Passeig de Gràcia

⑱ Casa Batlló

BUBBLES AND SPARKLES

⑲ El Nacional

Time for an aperitif? At ⑲ El Nacional ➤ p. 101 a former Art Nouveau car park has been transformed by Barcelona's flagship designer Lázaro Rosa Violán into an opulent, sparkling palace and hits just the right note.

⑳ Cervecería Catalana

Delicious Catalan tapas are served *a few steps further towards Carrer de Mallorca* at the popular ⑳ Cervecería Catalana ➤ p. 68.

SIP DRINKS LIKE HEMINGWAY

Follow Rambla de Catalunya towards Plaça de Catalunya, cross the square, and then walk down La Rambla. End the day with a drink at the legendary cocktail bar

㉑ Boadas

㉑ Boadas ➤ p. 98. Henry Miller and Ernest Hemingway both enjoyed a dry martini here.

❷ A STROLL THROUGH THE RIBERA QUARTER

➤ Well-heeled citizens and venerable craftspeople
➤ Genius artists and talented designers
➤ Street cafés and picnic spots

📍 Plaça de l'Àngel	🏁 Bar de l'Antic Teatre
➡ 3km	🚶 6–7 hrs (1–2 hrs total walking time)

ℹ️ Important tips: Monday is not a good day for this tour because many shops, galleries, bars, restaurants and museums are closed!

BARCELONA'S MOST BEAUTIFUL CHURCH

❶ Plaça de l'Àngel

❷ Santa Maria del Mar

From ❶ Plaça de l'Àngel *(Metro L4: Jaume I)*, the city's old wheat exchange, *turn down Carrer l'Argenteria*. Take a few moments for quiet reflection at ❷ Santa Maria del Mar ➤ p. 38, which many say is the most beautiful Gothic church in Barcelona. Head back into the foray outside and *walk along Carrer dels Sombrerers*.

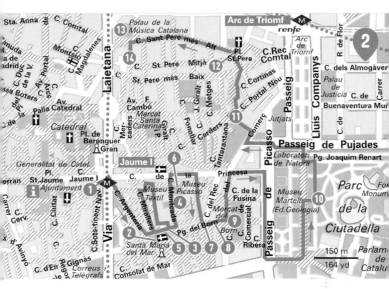

If you're in luck, the smell of hazelnuts and almonds will waft from the doors of the beautiful old grocery ❸ Casa Gispert ➤ p. 87 – a touch of 19th-century nostalgia!

❸ Casa Gispert

BROWSE & GRAZE

Take a few steps back and walk along the streets Mirallers and Carassa. Many lovely and creative shops have opened up in the old medieval houses of what used to be the historic centre of the textile and craftsmen's district. Browse to your heart's content in *the alleys along Carrer de la Barra de Ferro and turn onto Carrer Banys Vells before going left down the tiny street of Sant Antoni dels Sombrerers. Pass Placeta de Montcada until you come to* ❹ Carrer de Montcada with its ensemble of Gothic palaces – a gem of late medieval architecture. Most of the buildings now house galleries and museums, but before you tour the vast Picasso Museum, you should take a break for lunch and fuel up, e.g. on one of the delicious market-fresh veggie dishes at ❺ Petra *(closed Sun | C/ dels Sombrerers 13 | corner of C/ dels Banys Vells | tel. 933 199 999 | restaurantpetra. com | €).*

❹ Carrer de Montcada

❺ Petra

A LOT OF ART & A CROISSANT

After a good dose of fine art admiring the *Harlequin*, *Meninas* series and hundreds of other works in the Hunderten and ➏ Museu Picasso ➤ p. 37, you'll be ready for a coffee break. *From Carrer Princesa, head down the lovely little C/ dels Flassaders* with its charming shops and cafés. Keep an eye out for the small ➐ Pastissería Hofmann *(closed Sun afternoon | C/ del Flassaders 44).* Their croissants are legendary – choose plain or with a raspberry or marzipan filling.

➏ Museu Picasso

➐ Pastissería Hofmann

> **INSIDER TIP**
> Sweet sustenance

THE BEAUTY OF GREEN

At the end of C/ dels Flassaders, you will stumble upon the central ➑ Passeig del Born. Jousting tournaments were hosted here during the Middle Ages. A few very attractive façades have been preserved and restored. *Continue walking towards the unmissable* ➒ Mercat del Born, marked with a huge Catalan flag. Under the roof of one of the most beautiful historic market halls in Barcelona, you can see ruins from the time after the War of Spanish Succession. *Delve into the heart of modern Barcelona around the hall and down the side streets* filled with hip cafés and cool clothes shops, especially around Carrer del Rec. *Walk along Carrer del Commerç and then turn left on Carrer de la Princesa to take a little stroll through the popular* ➓ Parc de la Ciutadella ➤ p. 39. Families picnic on the grass, while street artists blow giant soap bubbles. *Exit Barcelona's favourite park at the main entrance on Passeig de Pujades. Return to Carrer del Commerç and then take Carrer dels Tiradors to one of the prettiest squares in the Old Town, the* ⓫ Plaça Sant Augustí Vell ➤ p. 36. It's also worth taking *a little detour along Allada Vermell*, which is lined with lovely pubs, bars and cabaret theatres.

➑ Passeig del Born

➒ Mercat del Born

➓ Parc de la Ciutadella

⓫ Plaça Sant Augustí Vell

Hip clothes shops abound near the Mercat del Born

EVERYDAY LIFE MEETS BOHEMIA

Walk along C/ de les Basses to one of the quarter's best, most atmospheric squares, the ⑫ Plaça de Sant Pere ➤ p. 35 with the Romanesque church Sant Pere de Puelles ➤ p. 36. Bask in the idyllic charm of this square on the steps in front of the church for a bit for an insight into everyday life before *heading down* Carrer Sant Pere més alt, the former centre of the Catalan cloth trade. At the end of the street, you will come across the unique Art Nouveau palace ⑬ Palau de la Música Catalana ➤ p. 35. Make sure to notice the impressive ornamentation on the façade, and inside is worth a peek too! After the day's walk and all that opulent Modernisme, relax and give your senses a rest in Bohemian style at the café ⑭ Bar de l'Antic Teatre *(Mon–Fri from 11am, Sat/Sun from 5pm | Carrer de Verdaguer i Callís 12 | tel. 933 152 354 | anticteatre.com | €).*

⑫ Plaça de Sant Pere

⑬ Palau de la Música Catalana

⑭ Bar de l'Antic Teatre

❸ TO THE TOP OF MONTJUÏC

➤ Museum hill: product of the 1929 World Exhibition
➤ Olympic dreams: the playground of star architects
➤ Paradise in a garden for romantics and art lovers

📍 Plaça de Espanya   🏁 La Tagliatella

🔄 7km   🚶 1 day (2–3 hrs total walking time)

ℹ️ Costs: approx. 46 euros (admission fees and cable car ticket)
Important tips: museums are closed on Sunday afternoon and Monday.

CULTURE AT THE FOOT OF THE MOUNTAIN

There'll be culture aplenty today. Our route for the day starts at ❶ Plaça de Espanya. It marks the entrance to the grounds of the international exposition that was held here in 1929. The main palace at the time, the

❶ Plaça de Espanya

Palau Nacional with its white domes and turrets, points the way. *Walk along Av. de la Reina Maria Cristina towards the escalators that go up to the Palau Nacional. Before the escalators, turn right on Av. de Frances Ferrer i Guàrdia* and you will find yourself in front of the spectacular art centre ➋ Caixa Forum ➤ p. 52, housed in a restored textile factory. Don't miss the top-class works of contemporary art inside. Located diagonally across the way, the faithfully reconstructed German expo pavilion ➌ Pavelló Mies van der Rohe ➤ p.52, a radically modern design and a sharp contrast to the splendour of Modernisme, has become an architectural icon.

Continue uphill past the open-air museum Poble Espanyol (see p. 53). *As the street curves, you will come to the* ❹ Olympic Stadium, which was originally built in 1929 and was completely renovated for the Olympic Games in 1992. The sports centre ❺ Palau Sant Jordi, designed by Arata Isozaki, resembles a tortoise shell, while Santiago Calatrava's radio tower, the ❻ Torre Calatrava, looks like a curiously shaped needle piercing the sky. Stroll behind the stadium through the Mediterranean world of the ❼ Botanical Gardens *(June–Aug 10am–8pm; April/May and Sept/Oct 10am–7pm; Nov–Jan 10am–5pm; Feb/March 10–6pm | admission 5 euros (combo ticket with Museu Blau 7 euros), free on Sun after 3pm and the f irst Sun in the month | C/ del Doctor Font i Quer 2 | jardibotanic.bcn.es).*

❹ Olympic Stadium

❺ Palau Sant Jordi

❻ Torre Calatrava

❼ Botanical Gardens

THRILLING VIEWS & INSIGHTS
The best way to get to the top of Barcelona's mountain (173m) is by the cable car ❽ Telefèric de Montjuïc. *Walk uphill along Carrer Doctor i Font Quer and Carrer dels Tarongers;* the station is located diagonally across from the Miró Foundation. The fantastic view from the gondolas is surpassed by the panoramic view from ❾ Castell de Montjuïc, an 18th-century fortress that now houses an exhibition that explains its eventful history. Hungry? Across from the lower cable car station, you can take a break for lunch at the *café-restaurant (Tue–Sat 10am–7pm | €€)* of the ❿ Fundació Joan Miró ➤ p. 54 amid colourful Miró sculptures before visiting the museum.

❽ Telefèric de Montjuïc

❾ Castell de Montjuïc

❿ Fundació Joan Miró

ROMANCE, ROMANCE &... MORE ROMANCE!
This section is for the romantics! *The way back down behind the Miró Foundation is no less exciting via the* ⓫ Escalera Generalife, an idyllic staircase with lush greenery and playful fountains. *These steps will take you down into the heart of the* ⓬ Jardins del Teatre Grec, the gardens surrounding the replica ancient amphitheatre Teatre Grec. In summer, you can sometimes catch a concert or a play here. If you can't wait that long, get up on stage and improvise a performance

⓫ Escalera Generalife

⓬ Jardins del Teatre Grec

⑬ Museu Nacional d'Art de Catalunya

yourself! *Passeig Santa Madrona will then bring you to the Palau Nacional with the* ⑬ Museu Nacional d'Art de Catalunya ➤ p. 54. The Romanesque frescoes are world famous. You can save the other parts of the exhibit for another time because your admission ticket is valid for two days within the same month!

EXPERIENCE A MAGICAL WATER SHOW

The tour ends at the Plaça de Espanya in the shopping and leisure centre Les Arenes, a former bull-fighting arena. Up on the rooftop terrace, there are several restaurants, such as the Italian ⑭ La Tagliatella *(daily | tel. 933 256 949 | latagliatella.es |€€).*From there, you can enjoy the view of the Font Màgica ➤ p.52, the "magical fountain" with its huge Art Deco water features and colourful lights that attracts hundreds of onlookers and their phones!

⑭ La Tagliatella

❹ SUN, SEA & SAND

➤ Boat trip through the old port
➤ Cycle ride through the historic fishermen's quarter on a Dutch-style bike
➤ Grilled sardines, olives – and canned sound

📍 Monument a Cristóbal Colom

🏁 Filferro

→ 6km

🚶 6–7 hrs (2–3 hrs total travel time)

ℹ️ Costs: approx. 25 euros (harbour tour, bike rental, admission fees, without food and drink)

TIME FOR A CHANGE OF SCENE

Begin your maritime exploration of Barcelona with a *40-minute boat tour* of the harbour on one of the popular and comfortable *golondrinas*, docked behind the ❶ Monument a Cristóbal Colom ➤ p. 50. Once you're back on land, *walk along the old harbour on*

❶ Monument a Cristóbal Colom

A rush of colours: the illuminated Font Màgica in front of the Palau Nacional

❷ Passeig de Colom and admire the swanky yachts anchored here. *The promenade passes by a colourful Roy Lichtenstein sculpture on the way to the Palau de Mar.* Inside this former warehouse, the ❸ Museu d'Història de Catalunya ➤ p. 49 offers an interactive trip through the history of Catalonia. Ready for a snack? Then the museum's rooftop terrace is just the place. Sit on the sofas at 1881 Sagardi *(daily 11am–midnight | gruposagardi.com)* and enjoy the fantastic panoramic view along with your late morning snack.

❷ Passeig de Colom

❸ Museu d'Història de Catalunya

CYCLE ALONG THE COAST
Follow Passeig de Borbó along the old harbour. Rent a Dutch-style bike at ❹ Donkey Republic *(Passeig de Joan de Borbó 2 | donkey.bike)* and explore the well-maintained promenade along the beach and the harbour. Download the app first.

❹ Donkey Republic

SAND UNDER YOUR FEET? INTO THE WATER

⑤ Beach

The ⑤ beach ➤ p. 51, water glistening, lies at the end of the promenade. To the right, a monumental sky-scraper shaped like a sail will grab your attention. It is the W-Hotel designed by Ricardo Bofill. *Keep to the left towards the Olympic harbour*, passing a sculpture by the German artist Rebecca Horn that involves a tower of rusty iron cubes. Lock up your bike well, take off your shoes and put on your flip-flops: on the stretch of beach in Barceloneta, you can enjoy beach life at its best. Swim in the Mediterranean Sea, soak up the sun or play a round of beach volleyball. Cycling is so much more fun once you're refreshed. Back on your bike, *cycle on* past a gigantic fish sculpture made of bronze ribbons – a creation of star architect Frank Gehry – and the tourist

Live your beach life at Barceloneta: stroll, swim and hop from beach bar to beach bar

hotspots of the Olympic harbour and stop for lunch at ⑥ Xiringuito Escribà ➤ p. 75, an admittedly not-so-cheap but very worthwhile paella paradise with a casual terrace right on the beach.

⑥ Xiringuito Escribà

THROUGH THE ALLEYS OF THE FISHERMEN'S QUARTER

To head back to town, take the promenade to Passeig Maritim and then turn onto Carrer de Sant Carles. The narrow streets, little squares and residents chatting under hanging laundry bring a charm all of its own to Barcelona's historic fishing village called ⑦ Barceloneta ➤ p. 48. Remember to return your bike first *(Passeig de Joan de Borbó)! Wander through the streets* and enjoy the maritime flair of this district. Keep your eyes, ears and nose open! Smells of freshly fried calamari? Happy laughter from behind an inconspicuous shop door? That means quality. *Now head back to Carrer de Sant Carles:* the rustic and lively ⑧ Bodega L'Electricitat *(closed Mon | C/ de Sant Carles 15)* is the place to go for a vermouth, the typical Catalan aperitif. With a bit of luck, you'll snag an atmospheric terrace seat at ⑨ Filferro *(Wed/Thur 4.30pm–midnight, Fri/ Sat 11am–1am, Sun 11am–midnight, closed Mon/Tue | C/ de Sant Carles 29 | tel. 932 219 836 | €)* and let your day at the sea work its magic.

⑦ Barceloneta

⑧ Bodega L'Electricitat

⑨ Filferro

GOOD TO KNOW

HOLIDAY BASICS

ARRIVAL

Air Flight prices have gone up since the pandemic; with a bit of luck you'll find return tickets from London from £50. Flight time from London is about two hours. Ryanair *(ryanair.com)* will get you cheaply to Girona (Gerona in Catalan), an approx. 90-minute shuttle bus ride from Barcelona (single 16 euros, return 25 euros). The major North American airlines also offer direct flights to Barcelona.

The Aerobus lines A1 (Terminal 1) and A2 (Terminal 2) take you into the city. The blue Aerobuses leave every 5–10 minutes to Plaça de Catalunya via Sants railway station and Plaça de Espanya and back *(5.90 euros, return ticket 10.20 euros, online purchase possible | approx. 30–45 mins | aerobusbcn.com).* If you are headed for the exhibition centre or the Zona Universitaria, you can also take metro line 9 into the city *(4.50 euros, approx. every 7 mins, journey time 30 mins).* From there, you can continue by metro to the city centre. Taxis from the airport charge a flat rate of 39 euros.

Bus Depending on your travel dates and departure location, you might find a cheap bus ticket. Most buses arrive at the main bus terminal *Estació d'Autobusos Barcelona Nord (C/ d'Ali Bei 80 | metro L1: Arc de Triomf | Eixample | ⑩ K/L9)*

Car The main route by car crosses the French–Spanish border at Ceret/La Jonquera.

Train Direct trains from Paris, Milan and Zurich arrive at the main station *Estación de Sants (Plaça dels Països Catalans 1–7 | metro L3, L5: Sants Estació | Sants-Montjuïc | ⑩ E7).*

How about a relaxed city tour by bus?

GETTING IN

British and US citizens need a valid passport for entry into Spain. Children need their own passport.

CLIMATE & WHEN TO GO

The best time to visit is in May/June or September/October, when the temperatures are pleasantly warm but not too hot. In late June, July and August the humidity levels are high, so it can get very sticky, and some shops and restaurants close for the summer or reduce their opening hours, while most of the city's inhabitants are on holiday and Barcelona is left to the tourists. Temperatures in winter seldom fall below freezing, and it's often possible to sit outdoors in the afternoon.

GETTING AROUND

BIKE

Spanning 308km, Barcelona's network of cycle paths is well developed. The omnipresent red and white *Bicing* rental bikes are only available to local subscribers. Visitors who enjoy cycling can rent a bike by the day or hour from one of many rental companies, e.g. *Happy Rental Bike (Av. Meridiana 28B | tel. 933 285 834 | happyrental bike.com | Sant Martí | ▥ K10)* or *Barcelona Rent a Bike (Calle Tallers 45 | tel. 933 171 970 | barcelonarentabike. com | Ciutat Vella | ▥ b1)*. All providers also offer e-bikes *(2 hrs from 12 euros)*.

BUS/METRO/TRAM

The best way to explore the Old Town is on foot. Otherwise, a cheap and fast way to get around is by metro, which runs between 5am and midnight from Sunday to Thursday and on public holidays, Friday to 2am and Saturday around the clock.

A single journey costs 2.40 euros, a carnet of 10 tickets (TMB Casual) 11.35 euros. For visitors, the Hola Barcelona Travel Card (2 days for 16.40 euros, 3 days for 23.80 euros, 4 days for 31 euros) pays off as it gives you unlimited access to the metro, trams and buses, including the metro trip to and from the airport. Children under four travel free. Buy online at hola barcelona.com for a ten per cent discount.

CABLE CAR

Cable cars guarantee added value for tourists – especially for children! A rack railway runs from the Paral·lel (L3) metro station (Funicular de Montjuïc | in the TMB fare system) to Avinguda de Miramar. From there, it's a cable car ✗ Telefèric de Montjuïc (March–May and Oct daily 10am–7pm; June–Sept 10am–9pm; Nov–Feb daily 10am–6pm | 9.40 euros single, 12.78 euros return, children 7.50 euros single, 9.18 euros return | telefericdemontjuic. cat) up to the top of Montjuïc. From the pier at the old port to Montjuïc you can take the aerial tramway Transbordador del Port (mid-Oct–Feb daily 11am–5.30pm; March–mid-Sept daily 11am–8pm; mid-Sept–mid-Oct daily 11am–7pm | 11 euros single, 16.50 euros return | telefericode barcelona.com).

(E-)SCOOTER

The (e-)scooter fever has gripped Barcelona, and a number of different providers are competing for the emissions-conscious, speed-loving clientele. Volkswagen subsidiary Seatmó (50–96 kmh, 0.28 euros/min. | seat.es/coches/seat-mo) offers a sharing service with more than 630 grey/ red scooters. These can be used between 6am and 2am. Acciona (up to 50kmh 0.31 euros/min; up to 80kmh 0.36 euros/min. | movilidad.acciona. com) operates 24/7, with prices for the red and white scooters staggered according to speed. Austrian company Cooltra (0.31 euros/min. | cooltra.com) has an app that provides information on where the scooters are. But watch out: pedestrianised areas are off limits, and a speed limit of 25 kmh is in place on cycle paths. Whatever you do, take your air pods out before you ride; the police make frequent checks and are strict in handing out 100-euro sanctions.

TAXI

Taxi fares are cheaper than they are in other cities. The basic charge is 2.30 euros, the price per kilometre is 1.21 euros on weekdays from 8am to 8pm, and 1.45 euros from 8pm to 8am and at weekends. The price for trips to the airport and cruise ship terminal are fixed at 39 euros. Hail taxis (green light: free) with your hand. Services such as *Cabify* and *Uber* are allowed to operate in Barcelona only on a very limited basis. You can book *eco-taxis* (electric or hybrid cars) by calling *tel. 932 783 000* or *tel. 605 584 539 (taxiecologic.com).*

EMERGENCIES

EMBASSIES & CONSULATES
BRITISH CONSULATE GENERAL
Av. Diagonal 477 | 08036 Barcelona | tel. 933 666 200 | ukinspain.fco.gov. uk | ☐ G6

US CONSULATE GENERAL
Paseo Reina Elisenda de Montcada, 23 | 08034 Barcelona | tel. 932 802 227 | es.usembassy.gov/barcelona | ☐ E3

HEALTH

In Spain, the European Health Insurance Card (EHIC) is accepted for EU visitors. Everyone else needs to take out an international health insurance policy that covers, among other things, the cost of repatriation.

In case of an emergency, head for a hospital A&E *(Urgencias)* or health centre *(Centro de Asistencia Primaria, CAP).*

EMERGENCY SERVICES

National emergency number: 112 | Local police numbers: 088 or 092 | fire: 080 | emergency doctor: 061.

At *tel. 112* and the main station of the *Policia Nacional (Via Laietana 43 | tel. 932 903 000 | metro L1, L4: Urquinaona | Barri Gòtic | ☐ b3)* there is an interpreter service available around the clock. Multilingual report forms are also available here and at all other police stations.

Credit card blocking hotline: *tel. 0049 11 61 16, Visa: tel. 900 99 11 24, Euro- and Mastercard: tel. 9 00 97 12 31.*

PICKPOCKETING

Pickpocketing is a serious problem in Barcelona, especially around the Ramblas, in Raval and on the metro. It's best to carry backpacks and bags in front of your stomach/chest and keep valuables separate from ID. If you're still caught out, head to the Catalan police *Mossos d'Esquadra*, especially if you can provide info on the perpetrator. The city's police force, the *Guardia Urbana*, won't investigate themselves, but will take a report and can be helpful for calls home. The Old Town police stations of the *Mossos d'Esquadra (Carrer Nou de la Rambla 76–78 | tel. 933 062 300 | tetro L2, L3: Paral·lel | Raval | ☐ a3)* and the *Guardia Urbana (La Rambla 43 | tel. 932 562 430 | metro L3: Liceu | Raval | ☐ b3)* are open 24/7 and can provide an interpreting service on request.

ESSENTIALS

ACCOMMODATION ONLINE

barcelona-online.com: tourist information, accommodation, last-minute offers, comprehensive service

barcelona-on-line.es: guesthouses, hotels and apartments, last minute too

hotelsbcn.com: hotel rooms

oh-barcelona.com: agency with hotel rooms and apartments on their books

BEACHES

The beaches along Barcelona's 4.5-km coastline are cleaned daily and are complete with lifeguards, toilets, showers and climbing frames for a carefree day at the beach. While the *Sant Sebastià*, *Barceloneta* and *Nova Icaria* sections in front of the Barceloneta fishing district and the Olympic Quarter have been taken over by tourists, further north, the beaches are still mostly local. The *Platja de Bogatell* is popular with Catalan families, while nudists congregate at *Platja de Mar Bella*. Technically speaking, nude bathing is allowed everywhere, but you will earn some critical looks if you don't stick to the nudist zone.

CITY CARD

A *Barcelona Card* is well worth buying if you are planning on using public transport (including the airport metro), as it becomes free of charge! And if you enjoy museums, it provides admission to 25 museums, including the Joan Miró Foundation, the Caixa Forum and the Picasso Museum. The card also offers discounts for two dozen attractions, including the main Modernist buildings. You can choose between two options: the *Barcelona Card Express* and the regular *Barcelona Card*. The former is valid for 48 hours and costs 19.80 for adults and children ages four and up. The *Barcelona Card* is valid for three to five days and costs between 43.20 (children 23.40) and 56.70 (children 36) euros. Get a ten per cent discount at *bcn.travel*, and you can exchange the voucher at a tourist office or on site – *BCN Travel (Mon–Fri 9am–6pm | C/ de Montsió 10 | metro L3: Catalunya | Barri Gòtic | f c2)*.

CUSTOMS

EU citizens can import and export goods for their own personal use without paying duty (e.g. 800 cigarettes, 90 litres of wine, 10 of litres spirits). If you come from other countries, e.g. the UK, USA and Canada, strict restrictions apply, such as 200 cigarettes, 4 litres of wine, 16 litres of beer, 1 litre of spirits or 2 litres of fortified wine. You may carry other goods up to a value of €300 per traveller or €430 for travellers by air and sea.

ENTRY FEES & TICKETS

Reserve concert and theatre tickets online via providers like *ticketmaster. es*, usually with a credit card. You can either print out the ticket or it is sometimes possible to pick up tickets at *Caixa Bank* machines (*caixabank.es | tel. 900 323 232*).

➤ Bargain hunters should head for *Tiquet Rambles (daily 10am–8.30pm |*

Rambla 99 | tel. 933 161 111 | metro: L3 Liceu | Raval | ☐ b2): Half-price tickets for same-day events are available at the Palau Virreina box office (starting three hours before showtime). But note that credit cards are not accepted! At theatres, opera houses and concert halls you can of course also buy tickets straight from the box office.

INFORMATION

Pre-trip information is available from the Spanish Tourist .
UK: 2nd Floor, Heron House, 10 Dean Farrar St, London SW1H 0DX | tel. 0207 317 2011 | spain.info
US: 60 East 42nd St, Suite 5300 (53rd Floor), New York, NY 10165-0039 | tel. 212 265 8822 | spain.info

The city's tourist office Turisme de Barcelona (barcelonaturisme.com) provides comprehensive information on what's available for tourists on its website. It also has several tourist information points, e.g., at Plaça de Catalunya, entrance to the Corte Inglés department store (daily 8am–8pm, incl. in English | tel. 932 853 834 | barcelonaturisme.com | metro L1, L3: Catalunya | Eixample | ☐ c1) or at Plaça Sant Jaume, in a side wing of the town hall, where there is also a selection of original Barcelona souvenirs (C/ Ciutat 2 | Mon–Fri 8.30am–8pm, Sat 9am–8pm, Sun 9am–3pm | metro L1: Jaume I | Barri Gòtic | ☐ c3). If you're on the hunt for information about worthwhile destinations outside the city, head for the Catalan government's tourist office (Mon–Sat 10am–8pm, Sun 10am–2.30pm |

Passeig de Gràcia 107 | Palau Robert | tel. 932 388 091 | gencat.cat/palau robert | metro L3, L5: Diagonal | Eixample | ☐ J7). For general information and practical advice, call the city hotline 010 (bcn.cat).

MONEY

You'll usually have to pay a fee to withdraw money from an ATM – in addition to the fees charged by your own bank! The amount should be displayed. Almost all restaurants, hotels and shops accept credit and debit cards, even for smaller amounts.

HOW MUCH DOES IT COST	
Coffee	1.60 euros for a café con leche
Shoes	from 14 euros for espadrilles
Wine	6 to 9 euros for 0.7 litres house wine
Cinema	from 8 euros for a ticket
Snack	4.50 euros for a serving of patatas bravas
Taxi	from 1.21 euros per kilometre

POST

Stamps can be bought at the post office (correos) or at a tobacco shop (estanc). The postage for cards and letters within Europe is 1.35 euros. The central post office (Mon–Fri 8.30am–9.30pm, Sat 8.30am–2pm | Plaça d'Antonio López | tel. 9 02 19 71 97 |

*metro L4: Barceloneta | Ciutat Vella |
c4)* is at the foot of Via Laietana.

PUBLIC HOLIDAYS

1 Jan	New Year's Day
6 Jan	Epiphany
March/April	Good Friday, Easter Monday
1 May	Labour Day
May/June	Whit Monday
24 June	St John's Day
15 Aug	Assumption of the Virgin
11 Sept	Catalan national holiday
24 Sept	La Mercè (patron saint of the city)
12 Oct	Discovery of the Americas
1 Nov	All Saints' Day
6 Dec	Constitution Day
8 Dec	Immaculate Conception
25/26 Dec	Christmas

TELEPHONE & WIFI

The country code for Spain is 0034 followed by the telephone number. When making a call from Barcelona dial 0044 for the UK; 0353 for Ireland, 001 for the US and Canada.

If you are planning on staying for longer or are making frequent calls, you can get a prepaid cell phone card in large department stores or the phone shops in the Old Town. Be prepared to show ID.

You can use the city WiFi free of charge (after signing up) at points marked with a blue "W" on the signs. See *ajuntament.barcelona.cat/barcelo nawifi* for an overview of the 650 or so hot spots. Most hotels and guest-houses now provide free WiFi as standard. More and more bars and cafés are also offering free WiFi for their customers.

TIPPING

In restaurants, hotels, etc., a tip of five to ten per cent is the norm. In bars and restaurants, the tip is placed on the little plate with the bill/check.

TOURS
BUS TOURS

Two companies in Barcelona offer sightseeing tours by bus, both departing from Plaça de Catalunya. The official municipal *Barcelona Bus Turístic (barcelonabusturistic.cat)* takes the blue route to important Gaudí buildings like the Sagrada Família, Park Güell and the Modernist Sant Pau hospital. The red route, meanwhile, focuses on areas near the sea and passes through Passeig de Gràcia, Diagonal, Sants, Montjuïc and the old port, the World Trade Centre and the Parc de la Ciutadella. You can switch between the routes. A day ticket costs 30 euros (children 16 euros). Book online for a discount. The double-decker buses have WiFi and an audio guide in 16 languages. Competitor *Barcelona City Tour (barcelona. city-tour.com)* also offers two routes: on the orange west route, visitors learn about the cruise terminal, Montjuïc and Camp Nou, while the green east route shows off the port areas and the main Gaudí monuments. Again, a day ticket costs 30 euros (children 16 euros) and changes are allowed. A book of discounts is also included.

HARBOUR TRIP

Explore Barcelona's old port or the Universal Forum of Cultures on a comfortable *golondrina* or aboard one of the new glass-bottomed catamarans that leave from behind the Columbus monument. *Tel. 934 423 106 | lasgolondrinas.com | metro L3: Drassanes | Raval | ▢ b4*

WALKING TOURS

Barcelona's Old Town is cramped and densely built, and so the city introduced restrictions on guided tours in the Old Town in summer 2022. In the maze of alleys in the former Jewish quarter of El Call, groups may not exceed 15 people, tours may only circulate in one direction, and loudspeakers have been banned, with tour guides facing sanctions for violations. While there are still so-called *Free Tours (freetour.com)*, i.e. tours where the guide(s) are paid a tip depending on how much you have enjoyed the tour, official city guides criticise the quality. Plenty of officially certified thematic tours on foot, by bike or Segway are available with *barcelonaturisme.com*, while *Icono Serveis (iconoserveis.com)* specialises in literary and cinematic routes.

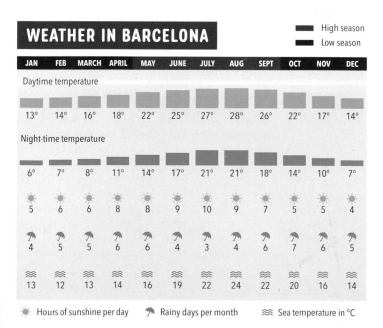

WEATHER IN BARCELONA

■ High season
■ Low season

	JAN	FEB	MARCH	APRIL	MAY	JUNE	JULY	AUG	SEPT	OCT	NOV	DEC
Daytime temperature	13°	14°	16°	18°	22°	25°	27°	28°	26°	22°	17°	14°
Night-time temperature	6°	7°	8°	11°	14°	17°	21°	21°	18°	14°	10°	7°
☀ Hours of sunshine per day	5	6	6	8	8	9	10	9	7	5	5	4
🐦 Rainy days per month	4	5	5	6	6	4	3	4	6	7	6	5
≋ Sea temperature in °C	13	12	13	14	16	19	22	24	22	20	16	14

☀ Hours of sunshine per day   🐦 Rainy days per month   ≋ Sea temperature in °C

WORDS & PHRASES
IN CATALAN

SMALL TALK

yes/no/maybe	sí/no/potser
please	sisplau
thank you	gràcies
Hello/Good morning/evening/night	Hola!/Bon dia!/Bona tarda!/ Bona nit!
Goodbye!	Adéu! Passi-ho bé!
My name is ...	Em dic ...
What is your name?	Com es diu?/Com et dius?
I am from ...	Sóc de ...
Sorry!	Perdona!/Perdoni!
Pardon?	Com diu?/Com dius?
I don't like this.	(No) m'agrada.
I would like .../Do you have ...?	Voldria .../Té ...?
May I ...?	Puc ...?

SYMBOLS

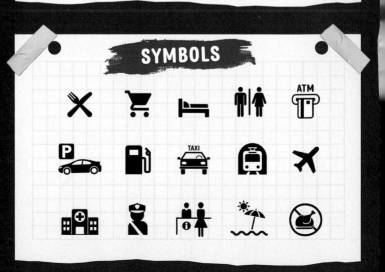

EATING & DRINKING

Could I please have ...?	Podria portar-me ...?
knife/fork/spoon	ganivet/forquilla/cullera
salt/pepper/sugar	sal/pebrot/sucre
vinegar/oil	vinagre/oli
milk/cream/lemon	llet/crema de llet/llimona
with/without ice/sparkling	amb/sense gel/gas
cold/too salty/not at all	fred/salat/cru
The bill, please.	El compte, sisplau.
bill/receipt	compte/rebut
tip	propina
cash/credit card	al comptat/amb targeta de crèdit

MISCELLANEOUS

Where is ...?/Where are ...?	On està ...?/On estan ...?
What time is it?	Quina hora és?
It's three o'clock.	avui/demà/ahir
How much is ...?	Quant val ...?
Where can I access the Internet?	On em puc connectar a Internet/ WLAN?
Can I take a picture here?	Puc fer-li una foto aquí?
Help!/Look out!	Ajuda!/Compte!
broken	trencat
breakdown/garage	avaria/taller
pharmacy/drug store	farmàcia/drogueria
fever/pain	febre/dolor
timetable/ticket	horario/bitllet
ban/prohibited	prohibició/prohibit
open/closed	obert/tancat
right/left/straight ahead	a la dreta/a l'esquerra/tot recte
more/less	més/menys
cheap/expensive	barat/car
(non) drinking water	aigua (no) potable
0/1/2/3/4/5/6/7/8/9/10/100/1000	zero/un, una/dos, dues/tres/ quatre/cinc/sis/set/vuit/nou/deu/ cent/mil

HOLIDAY VIBES

FOR RELAXATION & CHILLING

FOR BOOKWORMS & FILM BUFFS

📖 SIMÓN

Based on the turbulent life story of cousins Rico and Rico, young author Miqui Otero spins a fast-paced biography of Barcelona – from the Olympic Games to the present day. (2022)

🎥 VICKY CRISTINA BARCELONA

Star-studded comedy where two tourists (Scarlett Johannsen and Rebecca Hall) meet painter Juan (Javier Bardem) and his ex-wife (Penélope Cruz). Woody Allen sets an enchanting stage for the crazy web of relationships and the city. (2008)

📖 THE CITY OF MARVELS

Skilful portrait of booming Barcelona at the turn of the 20th century. Eduardo Mendoza's colourful classic takes us back to the World Exhibition and draws parallels with the present. (1986).

🎥 BIUTIFUL

This drama by Mexican star director Alejandro Iñárritu is no pretty portrait of the city. Terminally ill Uxbal (Javier Bardem) fights for his children's future in a Barcelona that tourists rarely get to see. (2010)

PLAYLIST ON SHUFFLE

0:58

❚❚ FREDDY MERCURY / MONTSERRAT CABALLÉ – BARCELONA
Incredible duet that became the anthem of the Olympics – a real earworm.

▶ MANU CHAO – RUMBA DE BARCELONA
The rhythm will have your feet tapping as soon as the lyrics hit your ears: *"Rambla pa'qui, Rambla pa'llá"*.

▶ ROSALIA – DESPECHÁ
Summer hit from the global Catalan flamenco singer who achieved stardom with reggaeton.

▶ JOAN MANEL SERRAT – MEDITERRÁNEO
The Catalan singer-songwriter's love song to his native region.

▶ GIULIA Y LOS TELLARINI – BARCELONA
Fast-paced title song to Woody Allen's *Vicky Cristina Barcelona*

Your holiday soundtrack can be found on **Spotify** under **MARCO POLO Spain**

Or scan this code with the Spotify app

ONLINE

BARCELONA-METROPOLITAN.COM
Information about the most important events of the month, insightful articles, tips and reviews – and much more.

BCN VISUAL
A must for before-and-after fans. This mobile app was developed by the city and shows historic images of both famous and little-known places to visit. Swipe between past and present with the augmented reality option.

GAUDI BCN
If you can't get enough of the genius architect's extraordinary creations, then this app from the tourism board can guide you to 11 emblematic buildings and provide detailed information direct to your ear at the touch of a button.

MAMMAPROOF.ORG
Mum knows best! All destinations, cafés and shops are tried and tested by experienced parents. If in doubt, check out their Instagram page.

TRAVEL PURSUIT

THE MARCO POLO HOLIDAY QUIZ

Do you know your facts about Barcelona? Here you can test your knowledge of the little secrets and idiosyncrasies of the city and its people. You will find the answers below, with further details on pages 20–25 of this guide.

❶ Which organisation protects the famous Catalan human castles?
a) UNESCO World Heritage list
b) Their own museum in Barcelona
c) The Spanish parliament

❷ How did Antoni Gaudí die in 1926?
a) He was killed by a stone falling from the Sagrada Família
b) He was hit by a tram
c) He was crushed by the crowd during a workers' protest

❸ What does Picasso's Cubist masterpiece *Les Demoiselles d'Avignon* show?
a) French governesses
b) Maids from Avignon
c) Prostitutes from Barcelona

❹ Where is the Catalan language still spoken apart from the east of Spain?
a) In Sardinia
b) In Malta
c) In Cyprus

❺ Which period do Barcelona's underground ruins date back to?
a) Bronze Age
b) Moorish times
c) Roman period

Beautifully blue: the inner courtyard of the Casa Batlló is magical

6 What led to a resurgence in the Catalan independence movement?
a) Most Catalans want a republic instead of a monarchy
b) The Spanish Constitutional Court curtailed the Catalan Statute of Autonomy in 2010
c) The Spanish Constitutional Court reintroduced bullfighting in Catalonia

7 What was the name of Gaudí's most important patron?
a) Eusebi Güell
b) Josep Batlló
c) Joan Pedrera

8 Which social class identified most closely with *Modernisme*?
a) The upper classes
b) The bourgeoisie
c) The workers

9 How does Barcelona's alternative crowd attempt to thwart prospective real estate tycoons?
a) With urban gardens
b) With loud concerts
c) With yellow ribbons

10 What is the stereotype of Catalans?
a) Hardworking entrepreneurs
b) Melancholic philanderers
c) Spirited sardana dancers

11 What is the city's former largest bullring now home to?
a) A theatre
b) A shopping centre
c) A hotel

INDEX

INDEX & CREDITS

WE WANT TO HEAR FROM YOU!

Did you have a great holiday? Is there something on your mind? Whatever it is, let us know! Whether you want to praise the guide, alert us to errors or give us a personal tip – MARCO POLO would be pleased to hear from you.
Please contact us by email:
sales@heartwoodpublishing.co.uk

We do everything we can to provide the very latest information for your trip. Nevertheless, despite all of our authors' thorough research, errors can creep in. MARCO POLO does not accept any liability for this.

PICTURE CREDITS
Cover photo: Park Güell, Detail (Schapowalow: A. Pavan)
Photos: AWL Images: M. Bottigelli (44/45); DuMont Bildarchiv: Pompe (50/51, 54); R. M. Gill (10); huber-images: M. Arduino (outer and inner cover flaps, 1, 4), P. Canali (14/15), H. - P. Huber (62/63 (© Salvador Dalí, Fundació Gala-Salvador Dalí/VG Bild-Kunst, Bonn 2017)), J. Lawrence (6/7), S. Lubenow (87, 118/119), F. Lukasseck (11), L. Vaccarella (148/149); Laif: M. Gumm (128); laif: F. Heuer (31, Laif: F. Heuer (89); laif: G. Knechtel (77, Laif: G. Knechtel (88); laif: N. Wohlleben (113); laif/hemis.fr: M. Borgese (73), F. Heuer (104/105); Laif/hemis.fr: L. Maisant (116/117); Laif/Le Figaro Magazine: Martin (102); laif/SZ Photo: J. Giribas (25); Laif/VWPics/Redux: I. Vallccillos (36, 99); J. Macher (151); mauritius images: M. Ramírez (21); mauritius images/age fotostock: Vallecillos (2/3), L. Vallecillos (26/27, 125); mauritius images/age fotostock/Clickalps SRLs (42); mauritius images/Alamy (8, 38, 78/79, 92, 133), R. Hamilton (56), Pjrtravel (22), Rosmi Duaso (91), M. Soler (17), Toniflap (46); mauritius images/Alamy/Alamy Stock Photos: T. French (75), G. López (12/13), S. Politi Markovina (64/65), A. Vorobev (59); mauritius images/Alamy/Alamy Stock Photos/AA World Travel Library (81); mauritius images/Alamy/Alamy Stock Photos/Stockimo: S. Race (70); mauritius images/Alamy/Alamy Stock Photos/Travelstock44 (69); mauritius images/Imagebroker: E. Bömsch (33), H. Dobler (60), M. Moxter (34/35); mauritius images/Photononstop (82/83); mauritius images/ Travel Collection: T. Langlotz (94/95); mauritius images/Westend61: M. Moxter (9); mauritius: C. Sámnchez Pereyra (107); mauritius/Alamy: C. Ehlers (108/109), P. Quayle (100), M. Soler (136/137), L. Vallecillos (114/115), A. Wilson (146/147); mauritius/ Cavan Images (110/111); Schapowalow/SIME: A. Serrano (134); Tupungato/Shutterstock.com (93).

5th Edition – fully revised and updated 2023
Worldwide Distribution: Heartwood Publishing Ltd, Bath, United Kingdom
www.heartwoodpublishing.co.uk

Authors: Julia Macher, Dorothea Maßmann
Editor: Christina Sothmann
Picture editor: Gabriele Forst
Cartography: © MAIRDUMONT, Ostfildern (pp. 120–121, 123, 127, 130, 135, inner flap, outer flap, pull-out map); ©MAIRDUMONT, Ostfildern, using data from OpenStreetMap, Licence CC-BY-SA 2.0 (pp. 8–29, 32, 37, 41, 47, 49, 53, 57, 66–67, 84–85, 96–97).
Cover design and pull-out map cover design: bilekjaeger_Kreativagentur with Zukunftswerkstatt, Stuttgart
Page design: Lucia Rojas

Heartwood Publishing credits:
Translated from the German by Madeline Taylor-Laidler, Kathleen Becker, Jennifer Wlacoff Neuheiser, Jozef van der Voort
Editors: Felicity Laughton, Kate Michell, Rosamund Sales
Prepress: Summerlane Books, Bath
Printed in India

MARCO POLO AUTHOR
JULIA MACHER

When Julia Macher moved to Barcelona in 2004, she was determined to finally get her driving licence. She still doesn't have one ... And thank goodness for that! After all, the city's pretty bars and cafés and the incredible buildings that suddenly come into view as you turn the corner are best discovered on foot.

DOS & DON'TS

HOW TO AVOID SLIP-UPS & BLUNDERS

DON'T BUY A MOJITO AT THE BEACH

At least, not one sold by a street vendor. The ingredients are stored in highly unhygienic conditions – we're talking in the gutter or under parked cars. The whole operation is banned, anyway.

DON'T WEAR A BIKINI TO THE SAGRADA FAMÍLIA

Religious and public buildings ask people to dress appropriately when visiting. But don't overthink it! You don't need to be completely buttoned up.

DON'T SIT DOWN AT A TABLE WITH STRANGERS

In Spain, the dinner table is an extension of the private sphere. As a rule, strangers don't take a seat, even if there are several spots free. You're better off taking a seat at the bar if you fancy small talk over an aperitif.

DON'T RAMPAGE THROUGH THE OLD TOWN

Budget airlines have transformed Barcelona into a party hotspot and a popular choice for stag dos and other alcohol-fuelled events. But the city's locals value their beauty sleep and won't take too kindly to hordes of drunken youths from western Europe.

DON'T COUNT EVERY PENNY WHEN SPLITTING THE BILL

In Barcelona, you pay Catalan-style (*pagar a la catalana*): the total is divided by the number of guests, regardless of whether the steak was two euros more expensive than the pasta. That said, if you only want a glass of wine, say so at the start and you'll be taken into account accordingly.